Table of Contents

From Exploration to Revolution

Expansion and Reform

America Today

Different Views of Earth

Geography is the study of Earth in all its variety. When you study geography, you learn about Earth's land, water, plants, animals, and people. One way to learn about Earth is to understand what it looks like. There are many ways to make a model of Earth.

Figures 1 and 2 show Earth like a globe. A **globe** is a true representation of Earth. It shows the round shape of our planet. Any one side of a globe shows only part of Earth. You have to spin the globe to see a different part.

A map shows Earth as though it were flat. There are many different kinds of maps. The map in Figure 3 tries to "open up" the round globe and show it as flat. With a flat map, you can see all of Earth at once. World maps and globes both show the same places. Look at the globes in Figures 1 and 2. Find some of the same places on the map in Figure 3.

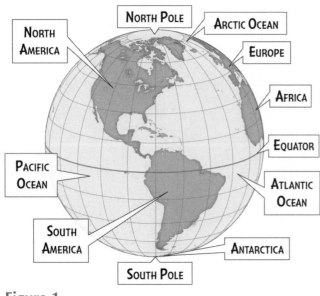

Figure 1

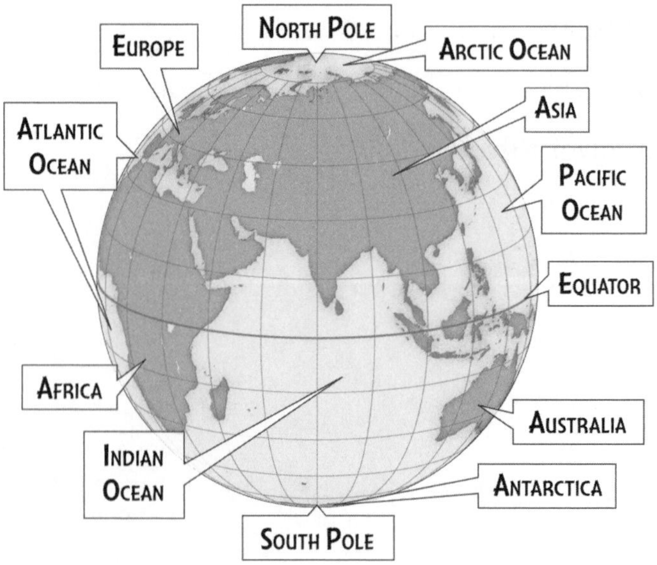

Figure 2

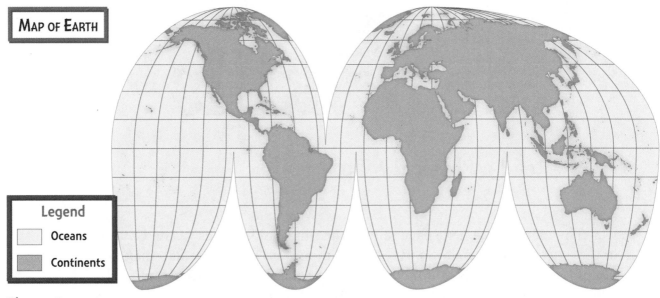

MAP OF EARTH

Legend
☐ Oceans
▨ Continents

Figure 3

Maps and globes show many things that pictures cannot. For example, find the equator in Figures 1 and 2. The **equator** is an imaginary line drawn around the center of Earth. The names of the seven **continents** and four **oceans** are also shown in Figures 1 and 2. You can also see the **North Pole** and the **South Pole,** which are the most northern and southern points on Earth.

Maps and globes have many uses. For example, what do you think a map or a globe can tell you about what it is like to live in a certain place? To start, consider that places near the equator have the hottest weather on Earth. The weather gradually gets cooler as you travel toward the North or South Poles from the equator.

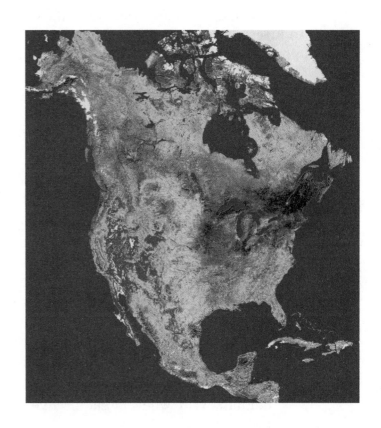

Another way to view Earth is from a picture taken from space by satellite. (A **satellite** is a device that orbits Earth.) These pictures are sent to Earth so they can be used to help predict the weather. Compare the photo at right with Figures 1, 2, and 3. Can you tell which continent appears in the photo?

Build Your

Read a Physical Map

The map on the next page shows the physical features of the United States, such as oceans, lakes, rivers, and mountain ranges. It also includes a **map legend** that tells you how to read the map. It has **symbols** or drawings, lines, or dots that stand for something else. The legend explains what each symbol on the map means.

A **compass rose** is a symbol that shows direction. The four main directions (north, south, east, and west) are called **cardinal directions.** **Intermediate directions** are halfway between the cardinal directions: northwest (NW), southwest (SW), northeast (NE), and southeast (SE).

A map's **scale** shows the relationship between distance on the map and distance on the ground.

The map also includes two smaller inset maps of Alaska and Hawaii. An **inset map** is a small map that accompanies a larger map and gives information that cannot be shown easily on the larger map.

Refer to the map and answer the following questions.

1. Along which part of the United States is the Pacific Ocean? Along which part of the United States is the Atlantic Ocean?

   _____

   _____

2. Which country borders the United States to the north? Which country borders the United States to the southwest?

   _____

3. Find the Great Lakes on the map and list them below.

   _____

4. In the left column of the table at the top of the next page, write the name of three mountain ranges shown on the map. In the right column, write whether each range is east or west of the Mississippi River.

Mountain Range	East or West?

5. Use the map to complete the table below.

River	The river flows in which direction?	The river flows into which body of water?
Missouri	east then southeast	Mississippi River
Columbia		
Ohio		
Arkansas		
Brazos		
Colorado		
Platte		

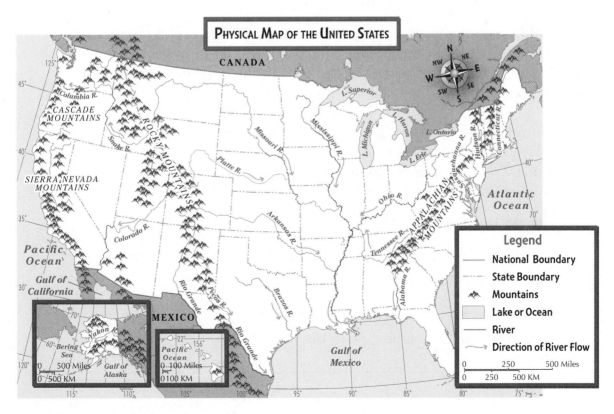

Explore North America

How do you think people traveled long ago without maps to guide them?

When the first people arrived in North America from Europe, the continent had not been divided into countries. In the area that later became the United States, there were no state boundaries. These people navigated from place to place mostly based on landmarks, or the physical features of the land.

Early European explorers of North America hiked across the land or floated on boats or rafts. Rivers were a good way to travel. Rivers could carry people downstream, sometimes for hundreds of miles. As you learned from the map on page 5, all rivers flow into another body of water such as a lake, an ocean, or another river.

In this activity, you will navigate across the United States from coast to coast just like these early people, though they did not have a modern map. You will begin your journey at the star on the northeast coast. You will end your journey at the star on the northwest coast.

1. Plan your trip by drawing lines on the map on the next page with a colored pencil. The lines you will draw will show the way you will travel. From the star on the northeast coast, draw a line southwest to the Appalachian Mountains in Ohio.

   The starting point (at the star) is between which two rivers?

   _____

   Which ocean lies to the east?

   _____

   What major water features lie to the north?

   _____

2. You decide to raft down the Ohio River. In which general direction will you travel? Into which river does the Ohio River flow?

_____

_____

3. From the place where the Ohio River ends, you decide to head northwest. Which two major rivers will you encounter as you cross the plains before you reach the Rocky Mountains?

_____

4. When you reach Idaho, follow the Snake River until it turns north. At this point, leave the river and continue traveling northwest.

Which mountain range will you encounter in Washington and Oregon?

_____

What river will you encounter before you reach your final destination?

_____

Into which body of water does this river empty?

_____

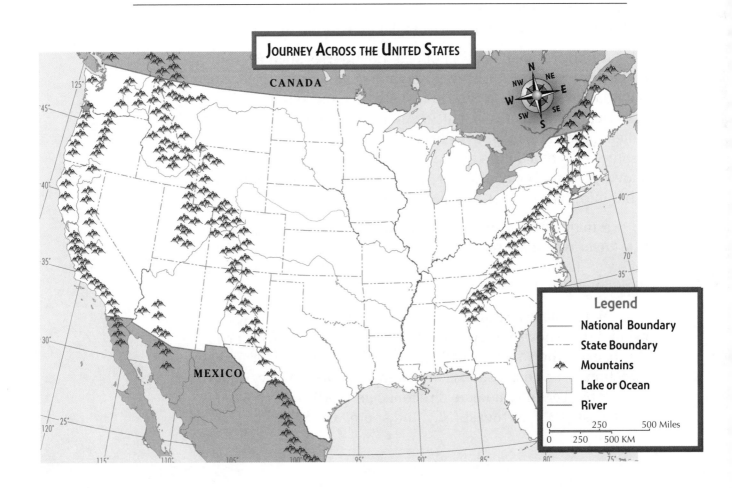

What Maps Can Tell Us

A **map** is a drawing of part of Earth's surface drawn to scale, as seen from above. It uses colors, symbols, and labels to represent features found on the ground. There are many different kinds of maps. We will discuss a few of them here. For additional information, see Appendix page 96.

The kind of map that is probably most familiar to you is a road map that is designed to show states, cities, and towns and the roads you can use to plan a trip. The map you used on page 5 was a **physical map.** A physical map shows mostly physical features of the land, such as rivers, lakes, and mountains.

A **political map** shows political boundaries such as countries or states. A **historical map** may show country or state boundaries at a certain time in history, or it may show a historical event such as a battle. Another common kind of map, called a **thematic map,** usually explains important facts about people. The map on the next page is a thematic map that also shows political boundaries such as state and country borders. What information does this map show?

A **map title** tells you what the map is about. A map with the title "Average Temperature in the United States" would give very different information than one with the title "Percent Change in Population for the 50 States, 1990 to 2000."

As you have already learned, a compass rose is a map symbol that shows directions. The four main directions (north, south, east, and west) are called *cardinal directions.* Intermediate directions on a compass rose are halfway between the cardinal directions. The intermediate directions are northwest (NW), southwest (SW), northeast (NE), and southeast (SE).

A map legend tells you how to read the map. It often has symbols or drawings, lines, or dots that stand for something else. The legend explains what each symbol on the map means. Sometimes, the legend has color codes that relate to the map. For example, the different colors on Map 1 show different rates of population change for groups of states.

A map's scale shows the relationship between distance on the map and distance on the ground. For example, one inch on a map might be the same as 10 miles on the ground. (This can be written as 1:10.) This means that to use the scale, you must measure between two places on the map with a ruler and then multiply that measurement to find the distance. For example, at a 1:10 scale, a measurement of 2.5 inches would be about 25 miles. Do all the states shown in Map 1 have the same scale?

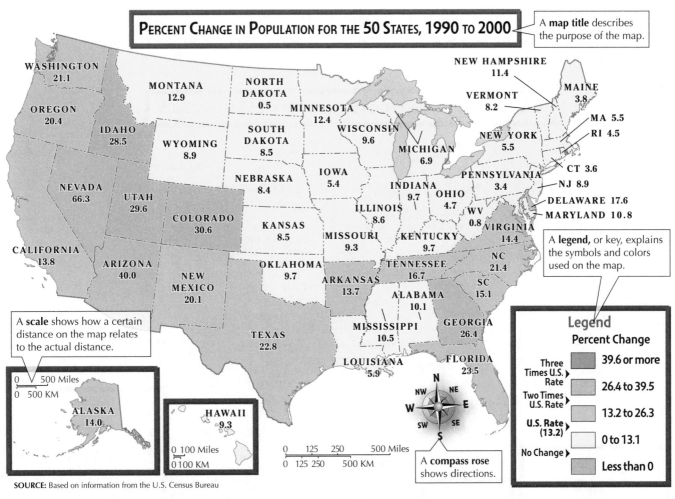

SOURCE: Based on information from the U.S. Census Bureau

Map 1

Build Your
Map Skills

Interpret a Population Map

Every 10 years, the United States conducts a **census,** or count of the U.S. population. A government organization, called the *U.S. Census Bureau,* does this. The last full census was conducted in 2000; the next one will be in 2010.

Based on the census information, the U.S. Census Bureau releases population estimates between full census years. The population estimate for 2005 is shown on Map 2.

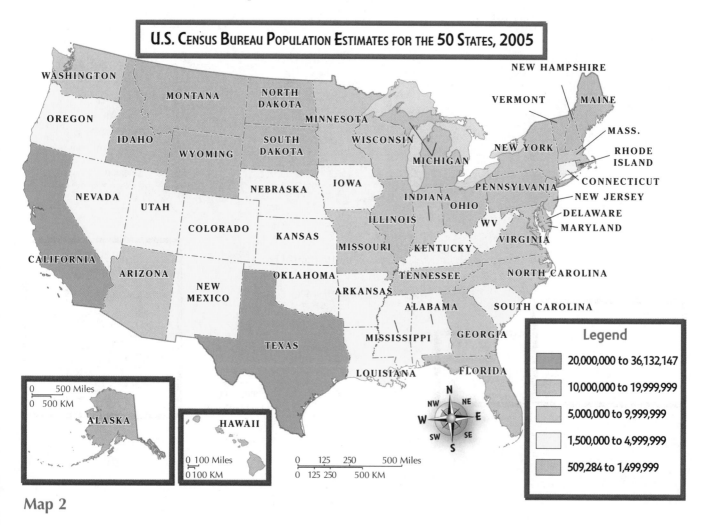

U.S. CENSUS BUREAU POPULATION ESTIMATES FOR THE 50 STATES, 2005

Legend
20,000,000 to 36,132,147
10,000,000 to 19,999,999
5,000,000 to 9,999,999
1,500,000 to 4,999,999
509,284 to 1,499,999

Map 2

The results of the full census are very important because the population of the country influences the way it is governed. For example, the number of representatives each state is allowed to send to the House of Representatives is determined by the state's population.

Refer to Map 1 on page 9 and to Map 2 on page 10 to answer the following questions.

1. Which two states have more than 20 million people? Use the compass rose to tell where they are located within the U.S.

_____

_____

_____

_____

2. Which two states experienced the fastest rate of population growth from 1990 to 2000? Use the compass rose to tell where they are located within the United States.

_____

_____

_____

3. What was the rate of population growth in the United States as a whole between 1990 and 2000? How do you know? Did most states exceed this rate?

_____

_____

4. Examine Map 1 carefully. What conclusions can you draw about population growth in the United States based on the map?

_____

_____

5. A classmate looks at Map 1 and tells you that Pennsylvania is one of the least populous U.S. states. Is your classmate correct? Explain why or why not.

_____

_____

_____

_____

Understand Data in Charts

How can data help you to learn about the people of the United States?

The U.S. Census Bureau has a big job! Besides counting the population, the U.S. Census Bureau collects many other types of information about people. This includes information about births, deaths, jobs, family income, housing, education, and the movement of people from place to place. This type of information, called **data,** is constantly changing.

The data from the U.S. Census Bureau are intended to give you a mental picture of the people of the United States. For example, over time, the number of people in certain age groups changes. Chart 1 shows the changes that took place between the years 1990 and 2000. Each age group in Chart 1 is shown as a percentage of the total U.S. population. Chart 2 shows the percentage of Americans age 25 and older who have graduated from high school or college. People under the age of 25 are not included in the data shown in Chart 2.

Refer to both charts to answer the following questions.

1. How many age groups are shown in Chart 1?

   _____

2. What is the youngest age group in Chart 1? The oldest?

   _____

3. In Chart 1, what do the brown bars show in each age category? What do the green bars show?

   _____

   _____

   _____

4. In Chart 2, what is the difference between the purple and blue bars? What is the first year for which data are given?

_____

_____

_____

_____

5. What percentage of people were ages 75 to 84 in 1990? In 2000? Did the population increase or decrease in that age category?

_____

_____

6. Based on the data, how would you say that the education level of Americans has changed over the past 60 to 70 years?

_____

_____

_____

Chart 1

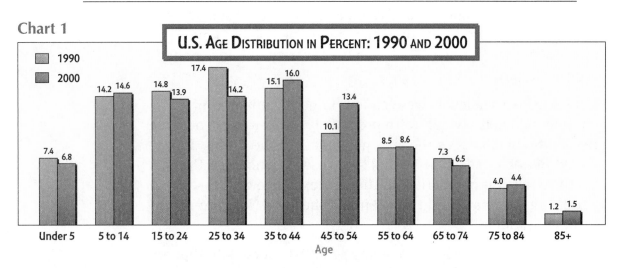

U.S. AGE DISTRIBUTION IN PERCENT: 1990 AND 2000

Chart 2

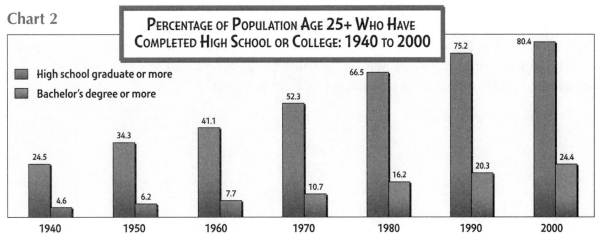

PERCENTAGE OF POPULATION AGE 25+ WHO HAVE COMPLETED HIGH SCHOOL OR COLLEGE: 1940 TO 2000

The Earliest Americans

Did you ever wonder in what kind of homes the first Americans lived or what kind of food they ate? Anthropologists and archaeologists devote their lives to answering such questions. **Anthropologists** are scientists who study all aspects of human beings, such as their society and culture. **Archaeologists** are scientists who use physical evidence and artifacts to analyze human cultures.

Scientists generally agree that no people lived in the Americas before about 12,000 years ago. Around 30,000 years ago, large **glaciers** (huge, slow-moving masses of ice) covered much of North America. Sea levels then were much lower than they are today.

Because sea levels were so low, large regions of the continental shelf—which were previously underwater—became dry land. This includes the area now beneath the Bering Sea. Called *Beringia* (see Map 1), this land bridge connected the northeastern tip of Siberia and the western edge of Alaska. People and animals could travel from Siberia to North America through Beringia.

About 12,000 years ago, many scientists speculate that an ice-free corridor, called the *Mackenzie Corridor,* had opened in the continental interior as the warming climate melted the great ice sheets. This allowed Paleo-Indians to migrate into North America from Siberia. Some scientists think that Paleo-Indians also used another travel route along the Pacific coast.

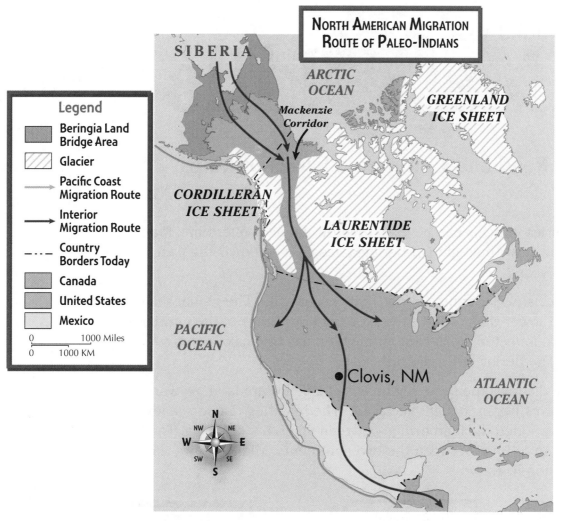

Legend

- Beringia Land Bridge Area
- Glacier
- Pacific Coast Migration Route
- Interior Migration Route
- Country Borders Today
- Canada
- United States
- Mexico

0   1000 Miles
0   1000 KM

SIBERIA

ARCTIC OCEAN

Mackenzie Corridor

GREENLAND ICE SHEET

CORDILLERAN ICE SHEET

LAURENTIDE ICE SHEET

PACIFIC OCEAN

•Clovis, NM

ATLANTIC OCEAN

N
NW   NE
W   E
SW   SE
S

Map 1

How do scientists know what happened so long ago? One way is by finding and studying what the ancient people left behind. One important archaeological site is at Clovis, New Mexico, where scientists discovered stone spear points next to the bones of large, extinct animals, such as bison and mammoth. This indicates that a group of Paleo-Indians hunted there. Named after the site where their tools were found, they are called Clovis hunters. The Clovis people hunted bison, horse, deer, elk, mastodon, mammoth, and small game. They also ate berries, nuts, seeds, and roots.

Clovis hunters stalk a wooly mammoth.

Build Your Map Skills

Read and Compare a Series of Maps

A series of maps can be used to show changes over time. Maps 2, 3, and 4 show how the region of Beringia has changed over the past several thousand years.

Map 2 shows Beringia about 12,000 years ago. The global sea level was much lower than today. This exposed large areas of the continental shelf and connected areas of Siberia with parts of Alaska not covered by glaciers. The Bering Strait did not exist.

Map 3 shows the same region about 2,000 years later, as warmer temperatures began to melt glacial ice. The resulting rise in sea level gradually flooded the land bridge between Siberia and Alaska. The Bering Strait began to form between the two continents. Map 4 shows the region's present shorelines.

SOURCE: Based on information from the U.S. Geological Survey.

Map 2

Spectrum Geography
Grade 5

16

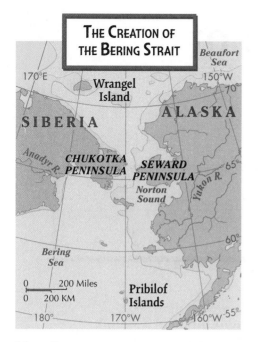

Map 3

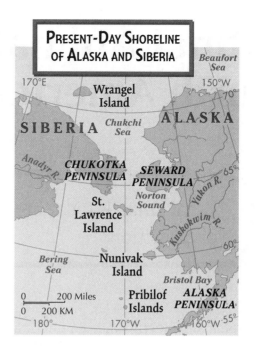

Map 4

Use the three maps to answer the following questions.

1. In which body of water is Wrangel Island located?

   _____

2. How did glacial melting affect the length of the Yukon River?

   _____

   _____

3. Besides the Bering Strait, name three new landforms caused by glacial melting at Beringia.

   _____

   _____

4. Besides the Bering Strait, name two new water forms caused by glacial melting at Beringia.

   _____

   _____

5. Look at Map 4. Between what two major lines of longitude is the Seward Peninsula? (If necessary, see Appendix page 97 for information about latitude and longitude.)

   _____

Extinct Animals of North America

What animals today are on the verge of extinction?

The Paleo-Indians in North America encountered a number of animals that are extinct today. A type of animal is said to be **extinct** when it no longer exists. Paleo-Indians hunted many of these animals for food. Other animals were hunters themselves.

Refer to Appendix pages 98–99 to find information to complete the following table on extinct North American animals. The left column of the table shows a picture of each animal. First, find the animal in the appendix and write its name in the table's second column. In the third column, write some information about the animal. For example, you could record information about its size, how it lived, how the Paleo-Indians interacted with it, or when and how it became extinct.

Extinct Animal	Name of Animal	Description of the Animal
	Ice-Age bison	This type of bison was almost twice as big as today's bison. Smaller bison took its place about 7,000 years ago.

Extinct Animal	Name of Animal	Description of the Animal

Now that you have completed the table, use the library to find the name of one North American animal that is currently endangered. (An **endangered** animal is in danger of becoming extinct.) Use the following worksheet to collect information about the animal you choose.

Name of animal: _____

Scientific name of animal: _____

Animal's characteristics: _____

_____

How endangered is this animal (how many are left)? _____

_____

Why is this animal endangered? _____

_____

_____

What is being done to help save this animal? _____

_____

_____

What Makes a Cave?

There are approximately 17,000 caves in the United States. A **cave** is a natural opening in the ground that is large enough for a human being to enter. Caves vary widely in size from a small room to an enormous cavern that extends underground for miles.

Caves have long been linked to human history. For example, early people used them for shelter. We know this because bones of human beings and animals have been found by archaeologists inside caves. Some cave walls are also decorated by art, called **petroglyphs,** drawn by early people.

How are caves formed? The process starts when rainwater mixes with carbon dioxide in the air and decaying material in the soil to create an acid. Over time, this weak acid in groundwater dissolves limestone and other types of rock creating cave passages. This process is shown in Diagram 1.

Petroglyphs provide evidence that ancient peoples once lived in caves.

How do scientists know where caves are? They often look for **karst,** a landscape that includes sinkholes, swallow holes, and disappearing streams. Karst is usually evidence of underground caves. A sinkhole is a place where the ground collapses. A disappearing stream is a stream that simply disappears into an underground cavern or swallow hole in the earth.

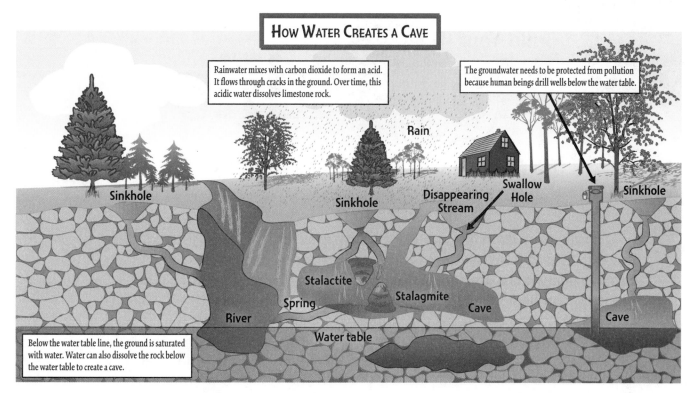

HOW WATER CREATES A CAVE

Rainwater mixes with carbon dioxide to form an acid. It flows through cracks in the ground. Over time, this acidic water dissolves limestone rock.

The groundwater needs to be protected from pollution because human beings drill wells below the water table.

Rain

Sinkhole

Sinkhole

Disappearing Stream

Swallow Hole

Sinkhole

Stalactite

Stalagmite

Cave

Spring

River

Cave

Water table

Below the water table line, the ground is saturated with water. Water can also dissolve the rock below the water table to create a cave.

Diagram 1

The exploration of caves is called **speleology.** Millions of people visit underground caverns each year to learn more about the science of caves and to see the beautiful rock formations, including stalactites and stalagmites that extend from cave floors and ceilings. Mammoth Cave in Kentucky and Carlsbad Caverns in New Mexico are among the most popular of these sites.

Stalactites extend from cave ceilings.

Why do we need to learn about caves? Scientists are particularly interested in caves because underground **aquifers** often form where caves are. Aquifers provide water to millions of people in the United States. For this reason, aquifers need to be studied and guarded against pollution. In addition, people need to know where sinkholes occur so they can avoid building on or near them. A sinkhole can destroy a building by undermining its foundation.

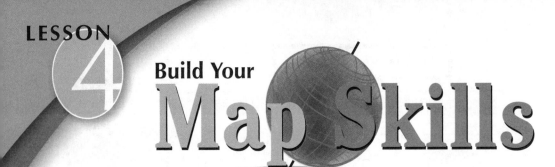

Build Your Map Skills

Read Geologic Maps

Mammoth Cave in Kentucky is the largest known cave system in the world. Natural processes took millions of years to create this cave system. This began when a great sea left large deposits of limestone rock over central Kentucky. Sandstone and shale were also deposited by an ancient river. When the sea and river disappeared, the sandstone and shale began to erode from flowing water. Around 10 million years ago, cracks and holes started exposing the limestone beneath. Water found its way underground, hollowing out the cave with underground rivers. Today, explorers have mapped more than 365 miles of passages in Mammoth Cave.

Refer to Map 1 and answer the questions below.

1. Name seven states that have large karst areas as compared to other states. Name three states that have almost no karst.

   _____

   _____

   _____

   Refer to Diagram 2 and answer the questions below.

2. What main geological features does the diagram show?

   _____

   _____

3. What types of rock are shown in the diagram?

   _____

4. How does groundwater get into the underground cavities?

   _____

5. How does the groundwater eventually leave the ground?

   _____

Legend

Karst

State Borders

0   250   500 Mles
0   250   500 KM

SOURCE: Adapted from the U.S. Geological Survey

Map 1

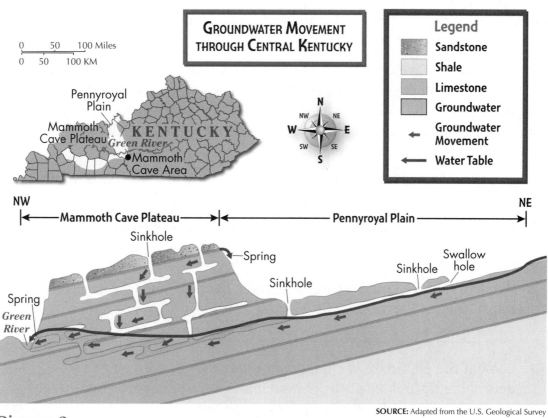

GROUNDWATER MOVEMENT THROUGH CENTRAL KENTUCKY

0   50   100 Miles
0   50   100 KM

Pennyroyal Plain

Mammoth Cave Plateau

KENTUCKY

Green River

Mammoth Cave Area

Legend

Sandstone

Shale

Limestone

Groundwater

← Groundwater Movement

← Water Table

NW

|← Mammoth Cave Plateau →|← Pennyroyal Plain →|

NE

Sinkhole

Spring

Sinkhole

Sinkhole

Swallow hole

Spring

Green River

SOURCE: Adapted from the U.S. Geological Survey

Diagram 2

Cave Dwelling Animals

Something to Think About

Why is it important to protect cave environments?

Caves provide shelter and habitat for many animals. There are three categories of cave-dwelling animals. **Trogloxenes** sometimes use caves for shelter but often dwell outside the cave environment. **Troglophiles** live most of their lives in caves but have the capability of living in other locations. **Troglobites** live only in caves and can't survive anywhere else. Over 200 species of animals live in Mammoth Cave alone.

The environment in caves is special. It doesn't change as rapidly as the outside world. The lack of light inside a cave limits plant growth and the availability of food.

Animals that live only in caves have adapted to their environment. The populations of cave animals tend to be small, and they usually have slow rates of growth and reproduction. The lack of light also has caused many cave animals to lack both pigment (they have no coloration) and sight.

Use the information above to answer the following questions about cave animals.

1. Why do you think the population of cave animals is usually small?

   _____

2. What advantage could a troglobite have over its cousins that live on the surface of Earth?

   _____

3. Look at the picture of each animal in the table. See if you can determine by looking at the animal if it is a trogloxene, a troglophile, or a troglobite. Write your answers in the table.

Animal	Animal Name	Trogloxene, Troglophile, or Troglobite?
	Raccoon	
	Blind crayfish	
	Camel backed cave cricket	
	Blind Texas salamander	
	Little brown bat	
	Blind millipede	
	Blind flatworm	
	Blind cave beetle	
	Adult cave salamander	

Exploring North America

The idea of exploring new lands sounds exciting. But European explorers of the fifteenth and sixteenth centuries faced many difficulties during their **expeditions,** or voyages of discovery. Because they usually journeyed to places no European had been before, most of them had no maps. They only had a general idea of where they were going, so they could easily get lost. Ships that crossed the Atlantic Ocean could be destroyed by sudden, violent storms. Starvation and disease were common.

Why did explorers take such risks to explore unknown lands? Most of them hoped to gain power and wealth. In the 1400s and 1500s, spices from Asia were highly prized in Europe, and the trade in them was profitable. However, the land route east from Europe to Asia was long and difficult. Europeans sought a shorter water route. Christopher Columbus reasoned that he could reach Asia by sailing west from Europe. At that time, he did not know that the Americas were in the way!

A voyage across the Atlantic was long and difficult.

The French were some of the first Europeans to explore the northeastern part of North America. Jacques Cartier explored the St. Lawrence River and northeast Canada. He was looking for a trade route to Asia. He brought stories back to France about the great wealth of Canada.

Samuel de Champlain followed Cartier to Canada, traveling up the St. Lawrence River to establish a fur trade with Native Americans. He founded the city of Quebec and explored Lake Huron, Lake Erie, and the New York region. Later, the French king sent him back to Canada to manage trade and also to find a route to Asia.

Jacques Marquette and Louis Joliet explored the Great Lakes, and they were among the first Europeans to explore the Mississippi River valley. They hoped the Mississippi River would lead to the Gulf of California and eventually to Asia. They wanted to establish a fur trade with the Native Americans. Marquette was a Jesuit priest who also wanted to teach Christianity. Their journey led to Robert de LaSalle's expedition down the Mississippi to the Gulf of Mexico. La Salle claimed the Louisiana Territory for France, including all the lands drained by the Mississippi.

Joliet and Marquette explored the Mississippi River by canoe.

Spanish explorers and soldiers were called **conquistadors.** They organized many expeditions across the southern part of North America. Ponce de León was the first European to travel along the coast of Florida. He claimed Florida for Spain and tried to establish a settlement there. Francisco Vásquez de Coronado searched the Southwest for Cibola, the seven cities of gold, hoping to take riches from Native Americans. He did not find the cities, but he was the first European to see much of the region.

Hernán Cortés was determined to take riches from the Aztec empire in Mexico. He conquered and destroyed much of their empire and took great riches back to Spain. Juan Rodriguez Cabrillo, a member of the Cortés expedition, explored the west coast of North America. He hoped to find a water route linking the Pacific Ocean to Hudson Bay.

The conquistadors sought riches from Native Americans.

Build Your
Map Skills

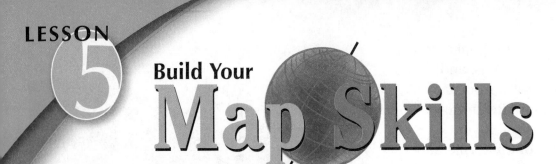

Read a Map of Exploration

The explorers of North America created the first maps of the continent. They returned to Europe with their maps and stories of their voyages. In some cases, their stories excited others and caused further exploration. Europeans' knowledge of the New World grew with each voyage of discovery.

The map on the next page shows important journeys of exploration to North America over a period of about 200 years. Because these journeys appear together on the same map, you can see all the expeditions at a glance and compare them.

Refer to the map and answer the questions below. When necessary, use the directions on the compass rose and landmarks to answer the questions.

1. Which explorer went on separate voyages representing two different countries? What were the countries? What areas of North America did he explore?

   _____

   _____

   _____

   _____

2. What similarities do you see in the areas that Cartier and Champlain explored? How did their voyages differ?

   _____

   _____

   _____

   _____

3. What area did Coronado explore in 1540–1542? Describe his journey as it appears on the map.

_____

_____

_____

_____

_____

4. Describe the important expedition that took place in 1524.

_____

_____

5. Who was the first European to see the Mississippi River? How can you tell this from the map?

_____

_____

_____

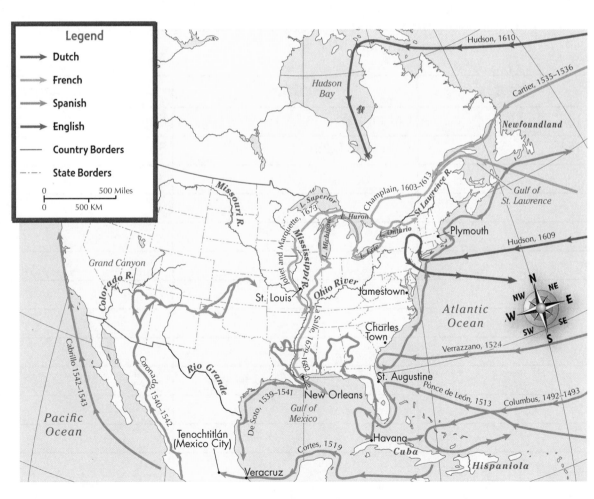

Make a Time Line

Something to **Think** About

Why is it important to know the order in which events occurred?

A **time line** can help to organize events in **chronological order,** or from first to last in the order in which they happen. This can help you to better understand the events and their importance.

Use the information from the map on page 29 to complete this time line. Write each explorer's name in the time line. When an expedition covers a range of years (for example, 1540–1542), put items in chronological order based on the first year in the range. The first two items have been completed for you.

Years	Explorer	Country
1492–1493	Columbus	Spanish
1513	Ponce de León	Spanish

Answer the following questions. If necessary, refer again to the previous pages of this lesson.

1. What were some of the dangers of a voyage of exploration to the New World?

_____

_____

_____

_____

2. What was the purpose of the Joliet and Marquette expedition?

_____

_____

_____

_____

3. What did the expeditions of Coronado and Cortés have in common? Were they successful? Explain.

_____

_____

_____

_____

_____

4. Select an expedition you have read about in this lesson. Do some library research to find more details about it. Answer the following questions about the expedition on a separate sheet of paper.

   • What was the explorer's name? Who sponsored or encouraged the expedition? When did it take place?

   • How many people went on the journey? How did they travel?

   • What was the goal or purpose of the expedition? Did the goal change during the explorer's travels? If so, how did it change?

   • The explorers traveled through what areas of North America?

   • What difficulties did the expedition encounter?

   • Why was the expedition important enough for later generations to remember?

Life on the Colonial Frontier

By the mid-1700s, the 13 American colonies along the eastern coast of North America had become home to people of many nationalities. At this time, the population of the colonies was growing very rapidly, mostly due to immigration. Most of these people lived east of the Appalachian Mountains.

Life was difficult along the colonial **frontier** in the mid-1700s. In 1763, the English and the French ended a long, terrible war, called the *French and Indian War.* With the English victory, France was forced to give most of Canada to the British. France also gave up claims to land west of the Appalachian Mountains, including the Great Lakes region and Ohio Country (see Map 1). However, the fighting did not end. Along the frontier, there was ongoing conflict between Native Americans and the English.

After the English victory in the French and Indian War, the English attempted to take control of the fur trade in former French lands in the Ohio Country and Great Lakes region. The Native Americans of this region had a long history of trading with the French. They had formed alliances (agreements or connections) with them. Some French traders had married Native American women. The Native Americans did not like the new English trading practices, and they were threatened by expanding English settlements.

British soldiers protected colonial settlements along the frontier.

French fur traders, called *voyageurs,* traveled the Great Lakes region.

The English did not understand the trading practices and traditions of the Native Americans. For example, they ended the French custom of gift-giving. This insulted many Native American leaders. The English also restricted the amount of gunpowder they would trade. This caused the Native Americans to become suspicious. Because of this, most of the tribes throughout the Ohio Country and Great Lakes region resented and feared the British.

Conflicts with the British caused an uprising of Native Americans in 1763 called *Pontiac's War*, named after one of the Native American leaders. Native Americans, including the Shawnee, Ottawa, Seneca, Miami, Wyandot, Chippewa, Huron, and other tribes, attacked English settlements and forts all across the frontier. They conquered Forts Sandusky, Michimilimackinac, Detroit, Presque Isle, and others. They also attacked Fort Duquesne much further east in western Pennsylvania.

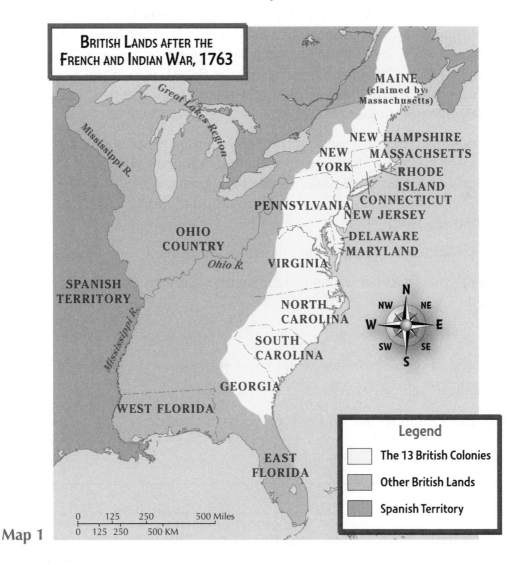

Map 1

Build Your
Map Skills

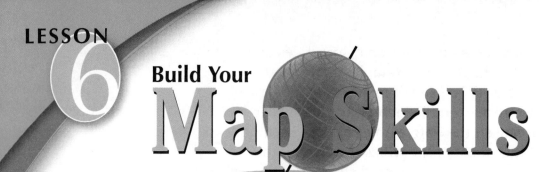

Conflict in the Colonies

After their victory in the French and Indian War, many colonists believed they had strong claims to most of the land up to the Mississippi River. These colonists were eager to move west and establish towns and trading posts.

As you have already learned, the Native Americans who lived along the frontier did not welcome the British, including the colonists. The British government wanted to make peace along the frontier to make it easier and less costly to defend it. To calm Native American worries that colonists would force them from their lands, the British issued the Proclamation of 1763. The Proclamation restricted colonial settlement west of the Appalachian Mountains.

Most colonists deeply resented the Proclamation. They thought they were entitled to move into these western lands. Colonists saw the Proclamation as another example of the British government's meddling in their affairs—a feeling of resentment that would build until it exploded into the Revolutionary War.

Refer to Map 2 and answer the following questions.

1. Describe the areas shown on the map where German immigrants settled.

   _____

   _____

   _____

2. Describe the ethnic makeup of the Southern Colonies.

   _____

   _____

   _____

3. Which ethnic group settled along the Hudson River?

   _____

4. Name two forts that were close to the Proclamation Line of 1763.

_____

5. Which Native American groups do you think would have been most immediately affected by the western expansion of the colonies? Why?

_____

_____

_____

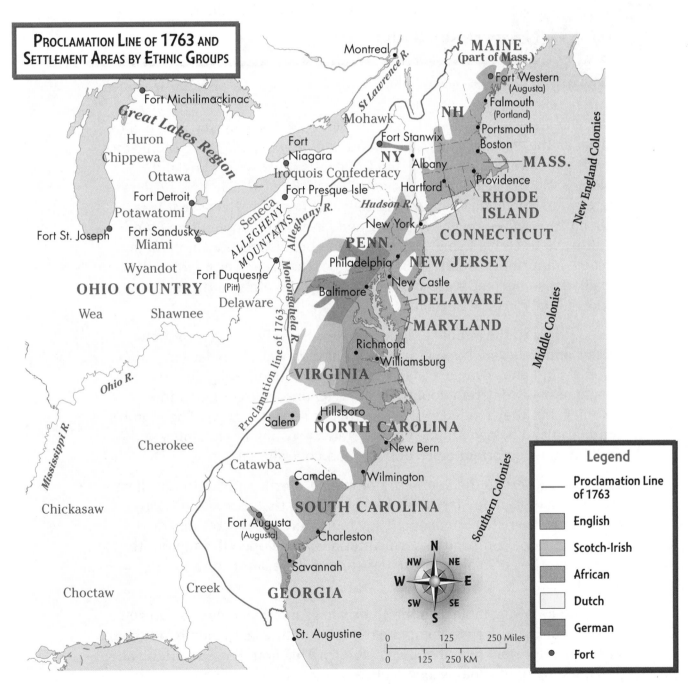

PROCLAMATION LINE OF **1763** AND
SETTLEMENT AREAS BY ETHNIC GROUPS

Montreal

MAINE
(part of Mass.)

Fort Western
(Augusta)

Falmouth
(Portland)

Portsmouth

Boston

NH

Fort Michilimackinac

Great Lakes Region

Huron

Chippewa

Ottawa

Mohawk

Fort
Niagara

Fort Stanwix

NY

Albany

St Lawrence R.

Iroquois Confederacy

Fort Presque Isle

Hartford

MASS.

RHODE
ISLAND

Providence

Fort Detroit

Potawatomi

Seneca

Hudson R.

CONNECTICUT

Fort St. Joseph

Fort Sandusky
Miami

ALLEGHENY
MOUNTAINS

Alleghany R.

New York

PENN.

Philadelphia

NEW JERSEY

Wyandot

Fort Duquesne
(Pitt)

Monongahela R.

New Castle

DELAWARE

OHIO COUNTRY

Delaware

Baltimore

MARYLAND

Wea

Shawnee

Richmond

Williamsburg

Proclamation line of 1763

VIRGINIA

Ohio R.

Hillsboro

Salem

NORTH CAROLINA

Cherokee

New Bern

Mississippi R.

Catawba

Camden

Wilmington

Chickasaw

SOUTH CAROLINA

Fort Augusta
(Augusta)

Charleston

Savannah

Choctaw

Creek

GEORGIA

St. Augustine

New England Colonies

Middle Colonies

Southern Colonies

N
NW NE
W E
SW SE
S

0   125   250 Miles
0 125 250 KM

Legend

Proclamation Line
of 1763

English

Scotch-Irish

African

Dutch

German

● Fort

Map 2

Learn More about the Colonies

 **Why is it important to learn about colonial life?**

The areas where the original thirteen colonies were settled became known as the *New England, Middle,* and *Southern colonies.* Massachusetts, New Hampshire, Rhode Island, and Connecticut were New England Colonies. New England colonists were largely English. The first settlers there came to America in search of religious freedom. Because it was difficult to farm the rugged New England lands, the people there found other ways to earn a living. Fishing and lumber, especially shipbuilding, became important industries. By the end of the French and Indian War, the area had also become a great center of trade. Boston was the most important city in New England.

Settlers to the Middle Colonies of New York, Pennsylvania, New Jersey, and Delaware hoped to make money, especially by farming. Many colonists in Pennsylvania, called *Quakers,* also sought religious freedom. People of many different countries and religions lived in the Middle Colonies, but they tended to live together in separate areas. The region's good farmland helped Middle Colony states prosper. Philadelphia and New York became important cities of trade and government.

The settlers to the Southern Colonies of North and South Carolina, Virginia, Georgia, and Maryland quickly learned that rice and tobacco would grow there in abundance. They found a ready market for these crops in Europe. Large farms, or plantations, developed throughout the South, and the colonists came to depend on slave labor to run the plantations.

The following table lists the 13 original American colonies. Do some research in the library to complete the table. In the last column, write at least one important fact about each colony. This could be something about the founding of the colony, one of its accomplishments, or the way of life that developed there.

Colony	Founded by	New England, Middle, or Southern?	Important Facts
Connecticut Year Founded: 1635	Thomas Hooker	New England	This colony created the Fundamental Orders of Connecticut in 1639, partly the basis for the U.S. Constitution.
Delaware Year Founded:			
Georgia Year Founded:			
Maryland Year Founded:			
Massachusetts Year Founded:			
New Hampshire Year Founded:			
New Jersey Year Founded:			
New York Year Founded:			
North Carolina Year Founded:			
Pennsylvania Year Founded:			
Year Founded: Rhode Island			
South Carolina Year Founded:			
Virginia Year Founded:			

The Road to Yorktown

During a long war, a single battle can sometimes be a turning point leading to victory. This was true during the American War of Independence in the year 1781.

In the spring of that year, General George Washington and his French allies were in New York making plans to attack the British forces led by General Clinton there. The French had just pledged additional forces to help the Americans. This was welcome news because the French army under General de Rochambeau was strong and well-supplied. The French navy could challenge the powerful British navy.

British major general Cornwallis commanded the British troops in the Southern Colonies. There, he conducted a **military campaign,** a series of battles against colonial forces. In May, Cornwallis moved his army from North Carolina into northern Virginia to receive reinforcements (additional troops) from New York. He attacked the Americans in Virginia. Cornwallis and about 8,000 troops then made their way to the small village of Yorktown on Chesapeake Bay to establish a naval base. There, the British could get supplies from the British navy.

In August, Washington learned that French admiral de Grasse was sailing to the Chesapeake Bay from Haiti in the West Indies. De Grasse had a large fleet of ships and more troops to help the Americans. Washington and Rochambeau planned to move their forces from New York to Virginia because de Grasse was coming to Chesapeake Bay, where he arrived on August 31. De Grasse blockaded the James and York rivers with some of his ships.

American troops marched south from New York to Virginia to engage the British.

Admiral Graves commanded a fleet of British warships. On August 31, his fleet left New York to fight the French at the Virginia Capes (off Chesapeake Bay). On September 5, Graves' 19 ships reached the Virginia Capes, where they fought the 24 French ships under Admiral de Grasse.

The French and the British fought a long battle, but the French finally drove away the British fleet. Graves retreated to New York on September 9. Now, Cornwallis could not leave Yorktown by sea because French ships controlled the bay. Also, Cornwallis could not receive more troops or supplies from the sea.

On September 10, French admiral de Barras arrived with additional French ships and reinforcements. His ships carried **artillery,** or large guns, to bombard the British positions. With Cornwallis cut off from the sea, American and French troops moved toward Yorktown. By September 30, they laid **siege** to the town, trying to cut off all means of escape or reinforcement.

Map 1

Build Your

Map Skills

Interpret a Battle Map

The Americans and the French arrived outside Yorktown on September 28. About 9,500 Americans and 8,800 French troops surrounded the British. On October 9, they began an artillery bombardment of Yorktown that destroyed much of the town and set fire to British ships in the harbor.

On October 14, French and American troops attacked the defensive positions of the British. Cornwallis tried to escape across the York River to his positions on Gloucester Point. However, he was kept from doing so by bad weather and a lack of boats. Realizing that he could not defend his position in the town, Cornwallis surrendered on October 19, 1781. His defeat eventually persuaded the British to abandon their attempts to control the American colonies.

Refer to Map 2 and answer the following questions.

1. Describe the major water features where the Battle of Yorktown was fought.

   _____

   _____

   _____

   _____

   _____

2. Describe the position of the French ships.

   _____

   _____

   _____

   _____

   _____

3. Where were the French and American troops positioned around Yorktown during the siege?

_____

_____

_____

_____

_____

4. Besides their positions at Yorktown, what other area did British, American, and French troops occupy?

_____

_____

_____

_____

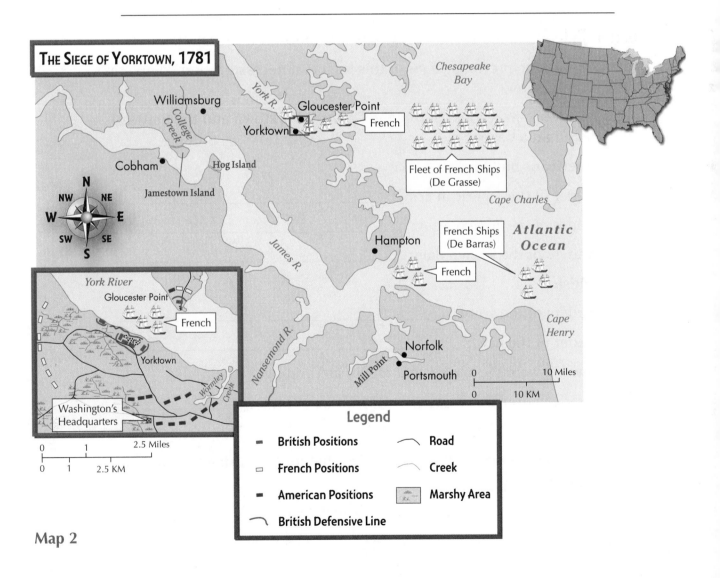

THE SIEGE OF YORKTOWN, 1781

Map 2

Organize Information

> How can organizing information help to increase your understanding?

The story of a historical event like a military battle can be complex and difficult to follow. As you have read, the Battle of Yorktown involved many people moving from place to place over a wide geographical area. To better understand the event, find a way to organize the information.

Refer to the previous pages of this lesson, if necessary, and complete the exercise below.

1. Who were the leaders during the Battle of Yorktown and the Battle of the Virginia Capes?

Americans and French

Leader of the American army: _____

Leader of the French army: _____

Leaders of the French navy: _____

British

Leaders of the army: _____

Leader of the navy: _____

2. How big were the armies that fought at Yorktown?

American army: _____   French army: _____

British army: _____

3. What was the size of the naval forces that fought during the Battle of Virginia Capes?

French navy: _____   British navy: _____

4. When and where were the battles fought?

Battle of Virginia Capes: _____

    Where: _____

Siege and Battle of Yorktown: _____

    Where: _____

5. Why did General Cornwallis move his troops to Yorktown?

_____

_____

6. Why did General Washington and General Rochambeau move their armies south to Virginia from New York?

_____

_____

_____

_____

7. What was the result of the Battle of Virginia Capes? Why was this battle important?

_____

_____

_____

_____

_____

_____

8. What was important about the arrival of the ships of Admiral de Barras at Chesapeake Bay?

_____

_____

_____

9. Overall, why was the Battle of Yorktown important to the American War of Independence?

_____

_____

_____

_____

Exploring the Louisiana Territory

In 1803, France grew tired of trying to establish an empire in the Louisiana Territory of North America. War with Britain seemed certain, and France was short of cash. President Thomas Jefferson was concerned about keeping the Mississippi River open to U.S. ships, so he made France an offer to purchase the city of New Orleans. France suggested that the United States buy all of the Louisiana Territory instead.

The massive new territory extended from Canada to the Gulf of Mexico and from the Mississippi River to the Rocky Mountains. The area was about 828,000 square miles and doubled the size of the United States. It cost about $15 million, a bargain for the United States.

President Jefferson wanted to organize an expedition to explore the new lands. He was eager to learn about the new territory and the possibilities for commerce there. He hoped the expedition could find a Northwest Passage, or water route to the Pacific Ocean. He also wanted to strengthen U.S. claims to Oregon Country by sending an expedition to explore that region. The president chose Meriwether Lewis to lead the expedition. Lewis chose William Clark as his partner. The exploration came to be known as the *Corps of Discovery*.

Lewis and Clark traveled up the Missouri River from St. Louis in a 55-foot keelboat that was specially built for them.

The Corps of Discovery began its journey in May 1804 and traveled for three years over an area that would later become eleven states. The expedition had many accomplishments. It acquired knowledge of the geography of the American West and mapped the new territory. In their journals, the explorers carefully observed and described dozens of plants and animals and made contact with Native Americans. The expedition also gave the United States a stronger claim to Oregon Country.

Lewis and Clark brought back descriptions of the buffalo and the grizzly bear.

At the time Lewis and Clark were on their journey, Zebulon Pike, a lieutenant in the U.S. army, also went on an expedition. His assignment was to explore the upper Mississippi River to find its headwaters. He was also to make sure that the British were not occupying American territory.

The following year, Pike headed a second expedition, this time to the southwest. Officially, he was to explore the headwaters of the Arkansas and Red rivers and to establish relations with Native Americans in the region. Secretly, however, his goal was to collect information about the presence of the Spanish in territory that was claimed by both the United States and Spain. Pike, essentially, was a spy for the United States.

In February 1807, Pike and his men were captured by the Spanish near present-day Santa Fe, New Mexico. The Spanish marched them south to the regional capital at Chihuahua, then north back to U.S. territory. This enabled Pike to travel through the region as a captive and to collect information. See Appendix page 100 to learn more about the successes and failures of Pike's expeditions.

Pike's Peak, near Colorado Springs, Colorado, is a reminder of the expedition of Zebulon Pike.

Build Your

Explorers of the West

Long before the cowboys and settlers, the Lewis and Clark and Zebulon Pike expeditions explored a vast land that was largely unknown and unmapped. The people on these expeditions had to be brave and strong to explore its mysteries.

The map shows the United States at this time of exploration. Refer to the map and answer the following questions.

1. Both the Lewis and Clark and the Pike expeditions entered areas claimed by more than one nation. Use the compass rose to describe the locations of these areas.

   _____

   _____

   _____

   _____

   _____

2. In which general direction did Lewis and Clark travel during the first year of their expedition? Which river did they follow when they left St. Louis?

   _____

3. In which direction did Pike travel in his 1805–1806 expedition? Which river did he follow?

   _____

4. Which U.S. states bordered the lands of the Louisiana Purchase? Which U.S. territories bordered it?

   _____

   _____

5. During their return trip in 1806, Lewis and Clark became separated for a time. Which one of them took the more northerly route?

_____

6. Use the compass rose and landmarks to describe the route of Pike's second expedition.

_____

_____

_____

_____

_____

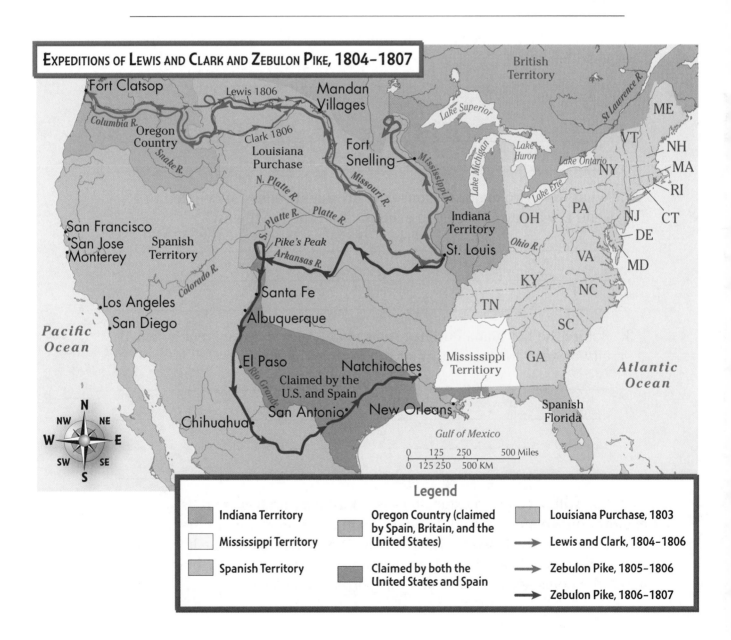

EXPEDITIONS OF LEWIS AND CLARK AND ZEBULON PIKE, 1804–1807

Legend

- Indiana Territory
- Mississippi Territory
- Spanish Territory
- Oregon Country (claimed by Spain, Britain, and the United States)
- Claimed by both the United States and Spain
- Louisiana Purchase, 1803
- → Lewis and Clark, 1804–1806
- → Zebulon Pike, 1805–1806
- → Zebulon Pike, 1806–1807

Defend the Louisiana Purchase

Something to **Think** About

Why is it important to debate the actions of the government?

Refer to the previous pages of this lesson, if necessary, and answer the questions below.

1. Why did France decide to sell the Louisiana Territory to the United States?

_____

_____

2. What were two major reasons why President Jefferson decided to send Lewis and Clark on an expedition to the Northwest?

_____

_____

_____

3. Before the Louisiana Purchase was made, why was the French-owned city of New Orleans important to the United States?

_____

_____

_____

_____

You will become an expert on the Louisiana Purchase and its exploration. To start, reread the material in this lesson and on Appendix page 101 about the Lewis and Clark expedition. Then, go to the library for further research. Read through at least one more source describing facts about the Louisiana Purchase and the Corps of Discovery.

Now, after your reading and research, you are ready to assume the role of someone just returning from the expedition with the Corps of Discovery. Some members of Congress are asking President Jefferson why the Louisiana Purchase was a good idea. They are wondering why Jefferson bought these lands that are so far away from settled areas. They ask, "How will the Louisiana Territory, a remote wilderness, benefit the United States?" They have also asked President Jefferson to explain the purpose of the Corps of Discovery expedition.

As a special assistant to President Jefferson, you must help write a persuasive argument. In the space below, explain why the Louisiana Purchase was a good idea. Describe why the new western lands are an asset to the nation. Describe the successful results of the Corps of Discovery expedition. Try to convince the skeptical members of Congress that the United States is better off with these new lands.

_____

_____

_____

_____

_____

_____

_____

_____

_____

_____

_____

_____

_____

_____

_____

_____

_____

_____

The Slavery Compromise

No issue has divided America like slavery. Slavery began in the South in the 1600s in Virginia and Maryland. Over a period of about 200 years, the labor of enslaved Africans became essential to the southern economy, which depended on agricultural products such as tobacco, rice, and indigo. In the 1800s, the invention of the cotton gin to process cotton caused an explosion of cotton planting in the South, increasing the demand for slaves.

In the 1800s, political forces in the North and the South clashed over the issue of slavery. People in the North tended to be against the practice of slavery. Some **abolitionists** called for the immediate end of slavery. Beginning in 1819, the nation's leaders planned a series of compromises. They feared that the slave states would **secede,** or leave, the United States. The slavery debate was about the status of slavery in the territories and the admission of new states to the Union as free or slave states.

The admission of Missouri to the Union created a crisis over congressional representation. In 1819, there were 11 free and 11 slave states. One more state on either side would upset the "free state/slave state" balance in the Senate. Missouri wished to enter the Union as a slave state. The Missouri Compromise allowed Maine to enter as a free state and preserved the balance in the Senate. As a further compromise, a line was drawn along the southern Missouri border. Slavery would be prohibited north of this line; south of the line, it would be permitted.

Senator Henry Clay of Kentucky was nicknamed "The Great Compromiser" because of his role in the slavery debate.

By the 1850s, southerners feared they would soon become a minority in Congress if additional free states were admitted to the Union. The debate this time was about whether to admit California as a free or as a slave state. In the Compromise of 1850, Congress did admit California as a free state. However, slavery was to be determined by popular vote in the territories of New Mexico and Utah.

In 1853, leaders in Congress wanted to organize a new Nebraska Territory to encourage settlement there. Southerners in Congress would not support their bill unless the Missouri Compromise was repealed. This repeal would allow slavery in the new territory. The Kansas-Nebraska Act of 1854 divided the new territory into Nebraska on the north and Kansas on the south. It was decided that each new territory would vote on the issue of slavery.

The Kansas-Nebraska Act inflamed the situation in Kansas. Violence soon erupted in the eastern part of the territory when antislavery and proslavery settlers poured into the area to support their own governments. By 1856, hundreds of people were killed and millions of dollars of property was destroyed. The territory was called *Bleeding Kansas*.

Over the next few years, the North and the South became further divided over slavery. After the 1860 presidential election of Abraham Lincoln, South Carolina was the first southern state to secede from the Union. In 1861, a group of southern states that had seceded from the Union declared themselves the *Confederate States of America*.

Abolitionist John Brown led raids against supporters of slavery in Kansas in 1856. In 1859, he led a slave rebellion at Harper's Ferry, Virginia.

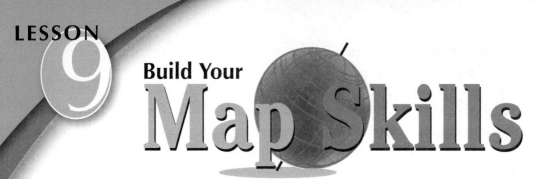

LESSON 9

Build Your Map Skills

Our Nation in Crisis

The maps tell the story of the debate and compromise that eventually led to the war between the North and South. Reread pages 50–51, if necessary. Refer to the maps, and answer the following questions.

1. At the time of the Compromise of 1850, how many slave states were there? How many free states?

_____

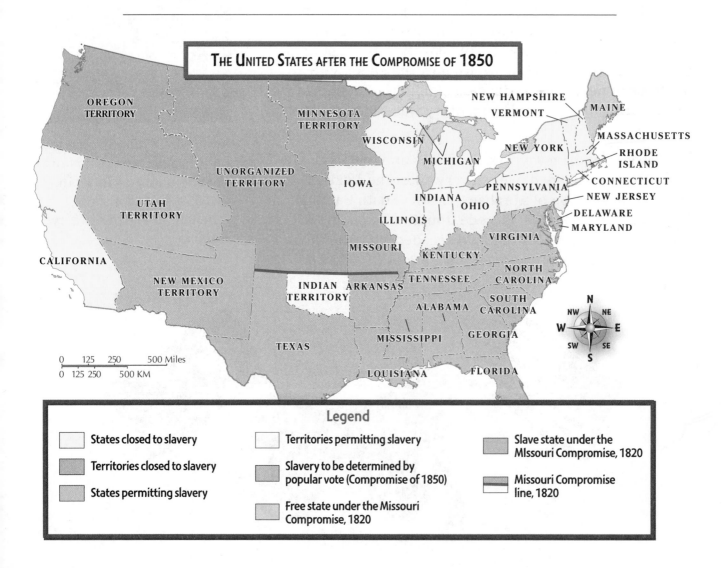

THE UNITED STATES AFTER THE COMPROMISE OF 1850

OREGON TERRITORY

MINNESOTA TERRITORY

NEW HAMPSHIRE

VERMONT

MAINE

WISCONSIN

MASSACHUSETTS

NEW YORK

RHODE ISLAND

UNORGANIZED TERRITORY

MICHIGAN

IOWA

PENNSYLVANIA

CONNECTICUT

UTAH TERRITORY

INDIANA

OHIO

NEW JERSEY

DELAWARE

ILLINOIS

MARYLAND

CALIFORNIA

MISSOURI

VIRGINIA

KENTUCKY

NEW MEXICO TERRITORY

INDIAN TERRITORY

ARKANSAS

TENNESSEE

NORTH CAROLINA

ALABAMA

SOUTH CAROLINA

N

NW NE

W   E

SW SE

S

TEXAS

MISSISSIPPI

GEORGIA

LOUISIANA

FLORIDA

0   125   250   500 Miles
0 125 250   500 KM

Legend

States closed to slavery	Territories permitting slavery	Slave state under the Missouri Compromise, 1820
Territories closed to slavery	Slavery to be determined by popular vote (Compromise of 1850)	Missouri Compromise line, 1820
States permitting slavery	Free state under the Missouri Compromise, 1820	

2. Name the slave states that were situated north of the Missouri Compromise line.

_____

3. What changes took place in the Unorganized Territory between 1850 and 1854?

_____

_____

_____

4. After the Kansas-Nebraska Act, which free states shared a border with at least one slave state?

_____

5. Was the Kansas-Nebraska Act a victory for southern slaveholders or northern abolitionists? How do you know?

_____

_____

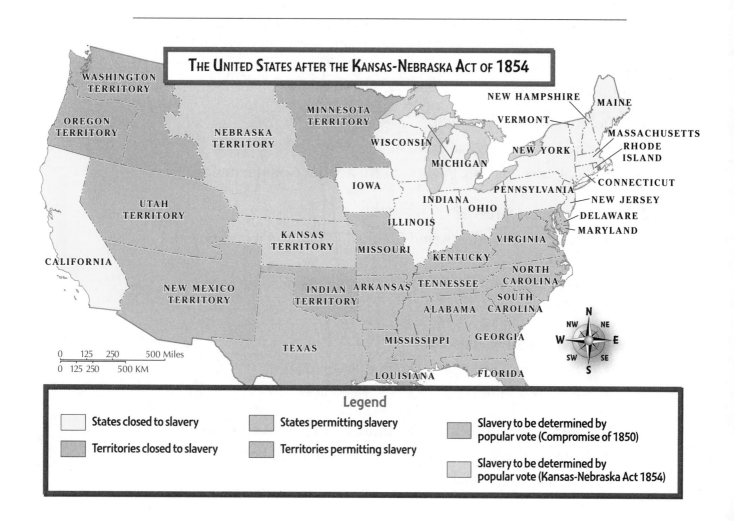

THE UNITED STATES AFTER THE KANSAS-NEBRASKA ACT OF 1854

Legend

States closed to slavery

Territories closed to slavery

States permitting slavery

Territories permitting slavery

Slavery to be determined by popular vote (Compromise of 1850)

Slavery to be determined by popular vote (Kansas-Nebraska Act 1854)

LESSON 9

Research Topics and People

Something to Think About

How can learning about history make you a better citizen?

Pick at least one important topic and one important person of the Civil War era from the lists below. To begin your research, refer to Appendix page 102 for an overview of the topic or person. Use the library to find out more information. Write your research notes on a separate piece of paper. Then, on a separate piece of paper, answer the questions below the topic and the important person that you selected.

Important Topics

The Fugitive Slave Act of 1850

- How did the Fugitive Slave Act come about?
- What effect did the Fugitive Slave Act have on the nation?

The Underground Railroad

- Describe the Underground Railroad. What was it and how did it work?
- Was the Underground Railroad dangerous in some ways? Explain.

The Emancipation Proclamation

- Who delivered the Emancipation Proclamation?
- Why was it important?

The Thirteenth Amendment to the United States Constitution

- Describe the purpose of the Thirteenth Amendment.
- What did it accomplish?

Important People

Henry Clay

- What was Henry Clay's job or role?
- Why was he nicknamed "The Great Compromiser"?
- Do you think he was successful or unsuccessful? Explain.

John Brown

- What was John Brown's cause?
- What did he try to accomplish? How did he try to accomplish it?
- Do you think he was successful or unsuccessful? Explain.

Dred Scott

- Who was Dred Scott?
- What did Dred Scott try to accomplish?
- Do you think he was successful or unsuccessful? Explain.

Robert E. Lee

- Who was Robert E. Lee?
- How did he get involved in the Civil War?
- What did he try to accomplish?
- Do you think he was successful or unsuccessful? Explain.

Abraham Lincoln

- What was Abraham Lincoln's job or role during the Civil War?
- What did he try to accomplish?
- Was he successful or unsuccessful? Explain.

Jefferson Davis

- What was the role of Jefferson Davis during the Civil War?
- What did he try to accomplish?
- Was he successful or unsuccessful? Explain.

Harriet Tubman

- Who was Harriet Tubman?
- What did she try to accomplish?
- Was she successful or unsuccessful? Explain.

A Growing Nation

Manifest **Destiny** was the American belief that the United States had a mission to grow and expand from the Atlantic Ocean to the Pacific Ocean. The phrase became popular in the 1840s to promote the acquisition of territory in what is now the western part of the United States.

In the period following the Civil War, miners and ranchers helped settle the West as they moved into the region seeking economic opportunities. Gold, silver, and other valuable minerals were found in many locations throughout the West. Growing cities in the North and East were great markets for beef, encouraging the growth of ranching in the West.

The U.S. government supported settlement on the Great Plains by offering any American the chance to own 160 acres of public land there after they lived on it for five years. This convinced many to try their hand at farming. Recent inventions, such as improved steel plows, seed drills, reapers, and threshing machines, helped make farming easier and more profitable. By the 1880s, the U.S. had become the world's leading exporter of wheat.

In the East, an abundance of accessible natural resources, such as iron ore, oil, and coal, helped fuel a manufacturing boom. A growing population provided a ready market for new goods, and technological advances fueled industrial expansion in the United States. Between 1860 and 1890, American inventions dramatically changed the way people lived.

During this same time, America's population more than doubled (from 31 million to almost 75 million). **Immigrants**—people who move from one country to another—flooded into America to work in the new factories.

Railroads crisscrossed the nation bringing raw materials to factories and goods to customers. But increasing industrialization created unhealthy and dangerous working conditions for many Americans, who labored long hours in factories for low pay.

Many immigrants to the United States arrived at Ellis Island in New York.

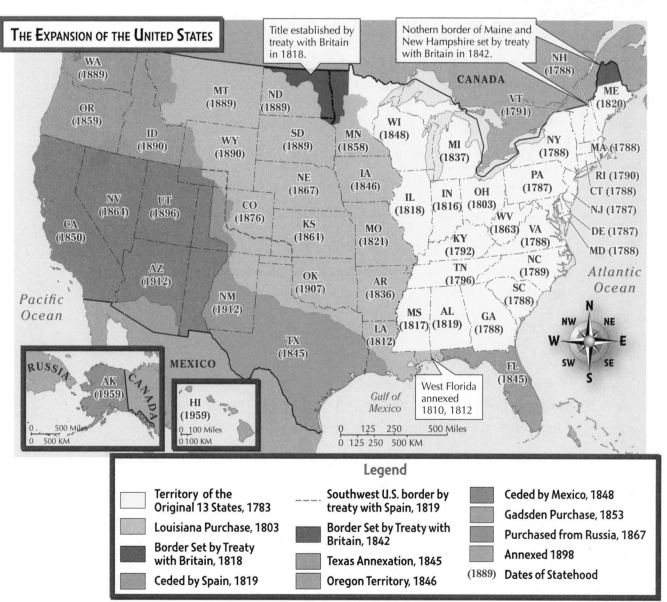

THE EXPANSION OF THE UNITED STATES

Title established by treaty with Britain in 1818.

Nothern border of Maine and New Hampshire set by treaty with Britain in 1842.

CANADA

WA (1889)
OR (1859)
ID (1890)
MT (1889)
ND (1889)
NH (1788)
VT (1791)
ME (1820)
SD (1889)
MN (1858)
WI (1848)
MI (1837)
NY (1788)
MA (1788)
WY (1890)
NV (1864)
UT (1896)
CO (1876)
NE (1867)
IA (1846)
IL (1818)
IN (1816)
OH (1803)
PA (1787)
RI (1790)
CT (1788)
NJ (1787)
CA (1850)
AZ (1912)
NM (1912)
KS (1861)
MO (1821)
WV (1863)
VA (1788)
KY (1792)
DE (1787)
MD (1788)
OK (1907)
AR (1836)
TN (1796)
NC (1789)
SC (1788)
MS (1817)
AL (1819)
GA (1788)
LA (1812)
TX (1845)
FL (1845)

Pacific Ocean

Atlantic Ocean

N
NW NE
W E
SW SE
S

RUSSIA
AK (1959)
CANADA

MEXICO

HI (1959)

West Florida annexed 1810, 1812

Gulf of Mexico

0 500 Miles
0 500 KM

0 100 Miles
0 100 KM

0 125 250 500 Miles
0 125 250 500 KM

Legend

Territory of the Original 13 States, 1783	Southwest U.S. border by treaty with Spain, 1819	Ceded by Mexico, 1848
Louisiana Purchase, 1803	Border Set by Treaty with Britain, 1842	Gadsden Purchase, 1853
Border Set by Treaty with Britain, 1818	Texas Annexation, 1845	Purchased from Russia, 1867
Ceded by Spain, 1819	Oregon Territory, 1846	Annexed 1898
		(1889) Dates of Statehood

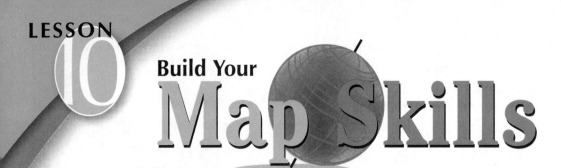

Build Your
Map Skills

The United States in 1900

In the late 1800s, the economy of the United States was able to expand largely because of its abundant natural resources. Natural resources provided the raw materials that businesses needed to make products. For example, because steel is made from iron ore, it was necessary to mine and transport the raw iron ore to manufacturing centers where it could be processed.

The map shows the major industries in the United States at the beginning of the twentieth century. Use the map to answer the following questions.

1. Identify the major industrial areas of the United States in 1900. Name five cities that were industrial centers in 1900.

   _____

   _____

   _____

2. Use the map to identify two states that had extensive forests in 1900. How do you know?

   _____

   _____

   _____

3. Identify the areas where steel and iron manufacturing were important. Name one steel- or iron-producing state.

   _____

   _____

   _____

4. Identify the parts of the United States where coal was mined. Name three coal-producing states.

_____

_____

5. Identify all states east of the Mississippi River where silver and gold mining took place.

_____

_____

6. How would you generally describe the states and their resources west of the Great Plains?

_____

_____

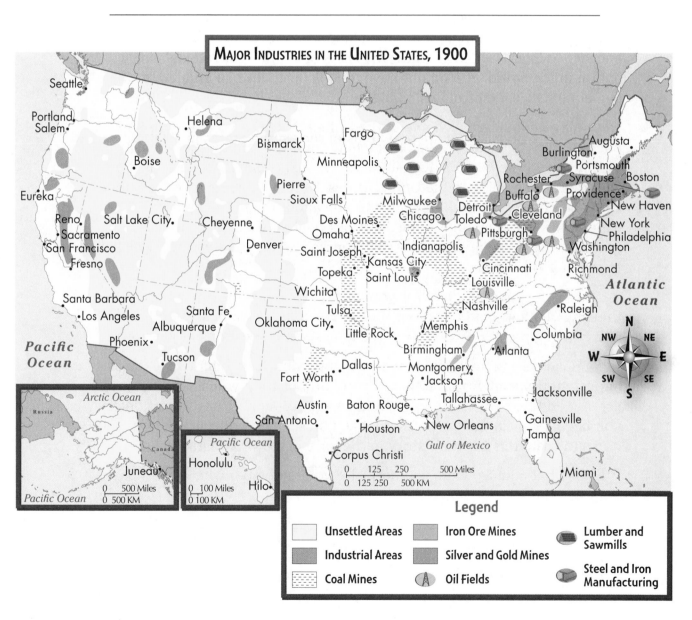

MAJOR INDUSTRIES IN THE UNITED STATES, 1900

Legend

☐ Unsettled Areas	Iron Ore Mines	Lumber and Sawmills
Industrial Areas	Silver and Gold Mines	Steel and Iron Manufacturing
Coal Mines	Oil Fields	

Take an Oral History

Something to **Think** About

Why is important to remember the past?

The United States is often called a *nation of immigrants.* As you have already learned, an immigrant is someone who moves from one country to another to live. The United States consists of people from almost every nation in the world. You do not have to look far to find an immigrant or someone descended from an immigrant.

Why do immigrants come to the United States? A good way to find out is simply by talking to them, listening carefully, and taking notes. An **oral history** is someone's account of a personal experience, such as the experience of coming to the United States, as remembered in conversation. Find someone who is willing to talk to you about their immigrant experience. This could be a neighbor or a relative such as a parent or grandparent. If you are an immigrant yourself, write your own story or talk to another immigrant.

To get a good oral history, you must prepare for the interview by thinking of a few good questions. Below are some questions you could use as a starting point. However, feel free to ask some questions of your own.

Make sure to make the person you interview feel comfortable. Most important, remember that to take a good oral history, you must be a good listener and take a genuine interest in what your subject has to say. Before you begin, explain that you wish to take notes. Later, you will use your notes to write this person's story in the form of a few paragraphs.

1. In what country were you born? Do you remember what it was like to live there?

   _____

   _____

2. What occupation did you have in your native country? Did you work at a job or go to school?

_____

_____

3. When did you come to the United States?

_____

_____

4. In what state and city do you live now? Why did you choose that place to live of all the communities in the United States?

_____

_____

_____

5. Why did you decide to leave your native country?

_____

_____

_____

_____

6. What do you miss about your native country? Do you still have relatives there?

_____

_____

_____

_____

7. What things have worked out best for you since you arrived in the United States? What things could be better?

_____

_____

_____

_____

8. Read through the answers to the questions above and any other oral history notes you may have taken. Write two or three paragraphs on a separate piece of paper about the immigrant you interviewed.

An Age of Reform

The rise of industry following the Civil War created some new problems for the United States. Many people thought that the nation needed a number of reforms. Important reform movements during this period involved woman suffrage, temperance, and child labor.

In July 1848, Elizabeth Cady Stanton and Lucretia Mott organized the first women's rights convention in Seneca Falls, New York. They demanded woman suffrage, or the right to vote.

The **suffrage movement** was opposed by many. Woman suffragists were accused of being wicked and unfeminine; some thought a woman's place was supposed to be "in the home."

After the Civil War, Congress introduced the Fourteenth and Fifteenth Amendments to the Constitution to protect the voting rights of African Americans. But women were not mentioned in the amendments. Some suffragists decided that a constitutional amendment for woman suffrage was needed. Others believed that the best strategy was to get state governments to pass woman suffrage laws.

Women of all ages gathered in public to demand a number of reforms, including the right to vote.

By 1912, nine states, including Washington, Oregon, California, Arizona, and Kansas had granted women full voting rights. Also that year, Theodore Roosevelt became the first presidential candidate to endorse woman suffrage. As more states granted women the right to vote, Congress began to favor a constitutional amendment. On August 21, 1920, the Nineteenth Amendment, guaranteeing women the right to vote, finally went into effect.

Another reform group, the Woman's Christian Temperance Union, believed that alcohol was hurtful to families. Its members thought that alcohol led to illness and the physical abuse of women and children. The **temperance movement** sought to limit or prohibit access to alcohol. In January 1920, the Eighteenth Amendment banned the manufacture and sale of alcohol.

The campaign against child labor became very emotional. Children had always worked on family farms. But in the new factories of urban America, children worked in conditions that were often unhealthy or unsafe. Accidents were common.

The National Child Labor Committee was formed in 1904 to campaign for the abolition of child labor. By 1914, all but one state had set a minimum age for employment. Many states also passed other limits on child labor, such as the maximum number of hours children could work. In 1916, the federal Keating Owen Child Labor Act outlawed the employment of children under the age of 14 in many factories.

Before child labor laws, many children worked long hours in factories and mines.

Build Your
Map Skills

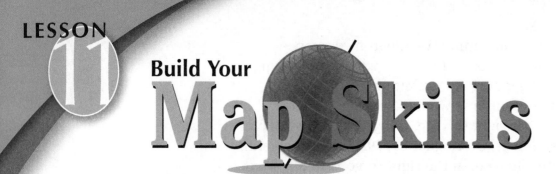

The Progress of Woman Suffrage

In the United States, woman suffrage was accidentally granted in New Jersey in 1776. New Jersey election laws had used the word *people* instead of *men,* so technically some women had the legal right to vote. This right was canceled in 1807, however. The movement for woman suffrage in America really began after the end of the Civil War.

By the late 1800s, American women had slowly begun to gain the right to vote. As more and more states and territories allowed at least partial suffrage to women, efforts to add a voting amendment to the U.S. Constitution gained momentum. The Nineteenth Amendment was finally ratified in the summer of 1920. The presidential election later that November was the first in which all American women were allowed to vote.

The map shows the state-by-state progress women made in their fight to gain the vote. Refer to the map to answer the following questions.

1. Which U.S. state or territory was the first to grant full woman suffrage? In what year?

   _____

2. Which U.S. states or territories had granted full woman suffrage before 1900?

   _____

3. Which U.S. states east of the Mississippi River had granted full woman suffrage before the passage of the Nineteenth Amendment?

   _____

4. Which U.S. states or territories west of the Mississippi River had granted full woman suffrage before the passage of the Nineteenth Amendment?

   _____

   _____

   _____

5. Generally describe the regions of the country where women did not have the vote before the passage of the Nineteenth Amendment.

_____

_____

_____

_____

6. When did your state grant woman suffrage?

_____

7. Use the map to determine what Iowa, Ohio, and Tennessee had in common regarding woman suffrage.

_____

_____

_____

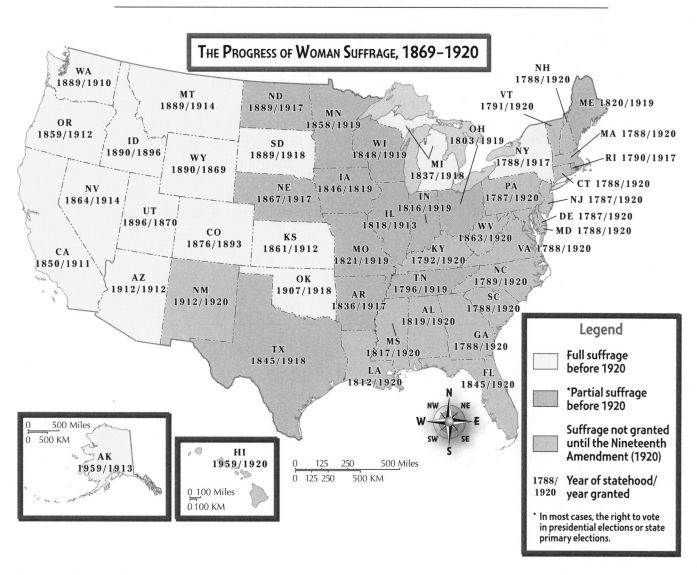

THE PROGRESS OF WOMAN SUFFRAGE, 1869–1920

WA 1889/1910
MT 1889/1914
ND 1889/1917
MN 1858/1919
NH 1788/1920
VT 1791/1920
ME 1820/1919
OR 1859/1912
ID 1890/1896
SD 1889/1918
WI 1848/1919
OH 1803/1919
MA 1788/1920
NY 1788/1917
RI 1790/1917
WY 1890/1869
IA 1846/1819
MI 1837/1918
NV 1864/1914
NE 1867/1917
IN 1816/1919
PA 1787/1920
CT 1788/1920
NJ 1787/1920
UT 1896/1870
IL 1818/1913
WV 1863/1920
DE 1787/1920
MD 1788/1920
CO 1876/1893
KS 1861/1912
MO 1821/1919
KY 1792/1920
VA 1788/1920
CA 1850/1911
AZ 1912/1912
NM 1912/1920
OK 1907/1918
TN 1796/1919
NC 1789/1920
AR 1836/1917
AL 1819/1920
SC 1788/1920
TX 1845/1918
MS 1817/1920
GA 1788/1920
LA 1812/1920
FL 1845/1920

AK 1959/1913
HI 1959/1920

0 500 Miles
0 500 KM

0 100 Miles
0 100 KM

0 125 250 500 Miles
0 125 250 500 KM

N NW NE W E SW SE S

Legend

Full suffrage before 1920

*Partial suffrage before 1920

Suffrage not granted until the Nineteenth Amendment (1920)

1788/ 1920 Year of statehood/ year granted

* In most cases, the right to vote in presidential elections or state primary elections.

Learn about Voting

What requirements will you have to meet before you are allowed to vote?

In the United States, you must be a registered voter before you are allowed to cast a ballot in an election. To become a registered voter, you must fill out a form provided by your state and meet certain requirements. For example, you can register to vote in Mississippi only if you have lived there for at least 30 days. If you qualify, you will be allowed to vote in upcoming elections.

The requirements for voting in the United States have changed over the years. As you learned earlier in the lesson, being male used to be a requirement. That has changed, as have other requirements. Do some library or Internet research about voting requirements to answer questions 1–3.

1. What was a poll tax? Which U.S. constitutional amendment abolished it?

   _____

   _____

   _____

2. What voting changes did the Twenty-sixth Amendment to the Constitution make? When was it ratified?

   _____

   _____

3. What common requirements for voting are shared by all states?

   _____

   _____

The table below shows national voter turnout in federal elections since 1980. Use it to answer questions 4–6.

4. What percentage of the voting-age population actually cast a ballot in the 2004 presidential election?

   _____

5. Why do you think voter turnout tends to rise and fall in four-year cycles?

   _____

   _____

6. Generally speaking, has voter turnout been increasing or decreasing since 1980 as a percentage of the voting-age population?

   _____

   _____

Voter Turnout in Federal Elections: 1980–2004				
[1]Year	Voting-age Population	Voter Registration	[2]Voter Turnout	Turnout of Voting-age Population (Percent)
2004	221,256,931	174,800,000	122,294,978	55.3
2002	215,473,000	150,990,598	79,830,119	37.0
2000	205,815,000	156,421,311	105,586,274	51.3
1998	200,929,000	141,850,558	73,117,022	36.4
1996	196,511,000	146,211,960	96,456,345	49.1
1994	193,650,000	130,292,822	75,105,860	38.8
1992	189,529,000	133,821,178	104,405,155	55.1
1990	185,812,000	121,105,630	67,859,189	36.5
1988	182,778,000	126,379,628	91,594,693	50.1
1986	178,566,000	118,399,984	64,991,128	36.4
1984	174,466,000	124,150,614	92,652,680	53.1
1982	169,938,000	110,671,225	67,615,576	39.8
1980	164,597,000	113,043,734	86,515,221	52.6

[1]Data for elections in the colored rows, such as 2004, were for president and members of Congress; elections in other years, such as 2002, were for members of Congress only.
[2]Turnout refers to the number of voters who actually cast votes.

Problems with Urban Growth

Since the 1800s, the Great Lakes region has been an important part of America's **economy.** The Great Lakes are a natural transportation system, and important natural resources like copper and iron ore were once plentiful there.

The millions of immigrants who settled in the Great Lakes region in the 1800s greatly impacted the land and water. Most of the mature forest was cut for lumber. The fur trade reduced the population of furbearing animals. Overfishing destroyed some fish populations. In the 1900s, the growing urban population and increased manufacturing created waste products that were dumped into waterways, polluting some of the Great Lakes.

In some cities, manufacturing has declined because of changes in the economy. Because of this, many old industrial areas have been abandoned. These areas are called **brownfields.** Because they are often polluted, people do not want to develop brownfields into new places for people to work or live.

Brownfields are abandoned industrial areas.

To avoid urban problems like crime, older housing, or traffic congestion, many Americans have moved away from cities into rural areas. But this migration has itself created problems including air and water pollution, higher energy use for homes and transportation, and the displacement of farmland and wild areas.

When people move into the country, they build more roads and parking lots, creating hard surfaces. Rainwater carrying oil, salt, and other pollutants quickly runs off these hard surfaces into creeks and rivers, damaging water quality. Water quality is also affected when people clear trees and other plants. This damage can warm streams, cause **erosion,** and kill fish.

A good **land-use plan** can help government officials ensure that important areas in a community are protected. Today, thousands of acres of wild land are protected in the Great Lakes region as state or federal forest land.

The U.S. Environmental Protection Agency also works with Canadian agencies to identify environmental areas of concern throughout the Great Lakes **basin** (see the map below). Agencies work together to develop action plans to clean up pollution and stop it at its source.

ENVIRONMENTAL AREAS OF CONCERN (AOCs) IN THE GREAT LAKES BASIN

Legend
- United States AOCs
- Canadian AOCs
- Binational AOCs

SOURCE: Environmental Protection Agency

Build Your
Map Skills

Study a Map of Urban Growth

The Great Lakes basin includes areas of Canada as well as the United States. Today, state and federal governments in both countries try to work together to solve water pollution problems along the border.

To control water pollution, conservationists must identify **watersheds.** These include the large rivers that drain an area and their **tributaries,** or the smaller streams that flow into them. The map and table provide information about the watersheds in southeastern Michigan and part of Canada. The map also shows the progress of urban growth in the area of greater Detroit.

Use the map and table to answer the following questions.

1. Which river shown on the map has the largest watershed area? Into which body of water does this river flow?

   _____

   _____

2. Which river shown on the map has the smallest watershed area? In which Michigan county is this river located? This river is a tributary of which larger river?

   _____

   _____

3. Name three Michigan counties that are at least partially drained by the River Raisin watershed.

   _____

4. Which two counties in southeastern Michigan are projected to have the least amount of urban area by 2020?

   _____

5. In which general direction is urban growth spreading most quickly in southeastern Michigan?

   _____

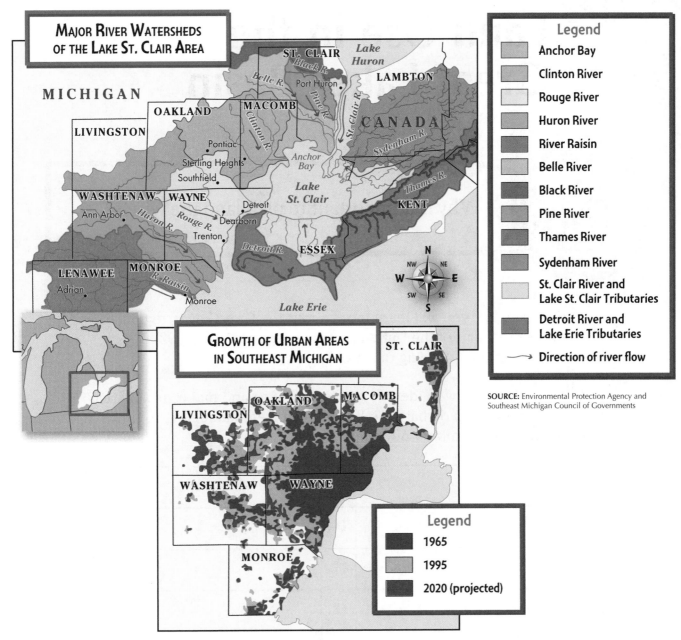

MAJOR RIVER WATERSHEDS OF THE LAKE ST. CLAIR AREA

MICHIGAN

LIVINGSTON

OAKLAND

Pontiac
Sterling Heights
Southfield

WASHTENAW   WAYNE

Ann Arbor   Huron R.   Rouge R.
Detroit
Dearborn
Trenton

LENAWEE   MONROE

Adrian   R. Raisin

Monroe

ST. CLAIR
Black R.
Port Huron
Pine R.   Belle R.
MACOMB
Clinton R.

LAMBTON

CANADA

St. Clair R.

Anchor Bay

Lake St. Clair

Sydenham R.

Thames R.

KENT

Detroit R.   ESSEX

Lake Erie

Lake Huron

Legend

	Anchor Bay
	Clinton River
	Rouge River
	Huron River
	River Raisin
	Belle River
	Black River
	Pine River
	Thames River
	Sydenham River
	St. Clair River and Lake St. Clair Tributaries
	Detroit River and Lake Erie Tributaries
→	Direction of river flow

SOURCE: Environmental Protection Agency and Southeast Michigan Council of Governments

GROWTH OF URBAN AREAS IN SOUTHEAST MICHIGAN

ST. CLAIR

LIVINGSTON   OAKLAND   MACOMB

WASHTENAW   WAYNE

MONROE

Legend

	1965
	1995
	2020 (projected)

River	Watershed Area (in square miles)	Primary Watershed Land Use
Black River	746	Agricultural
Pine River	135	Agricultural
Belle River	971	Agricultural
Sydenham River	938	Agricultural
Thames River	2,234	Agricultural and Urban
Clinton River	760	Urban, Suburban, and Rural
Rouge River	467	Urban
Huron River	900	Urban, Suburban, and Rural
River Raisin	1,070	Agricultural

Land Use in the Great Lakes Basin

Something to **Think** About

Why is it important to plan land use wisely?

In this exercise, you will learn more about the Great Lakes region. If necessary, use the map of the United States on Appendix page 92 for reference. Answer the following questions.

1. Use the table below to identify the Great Lakes and major urban areas shown on the map on page 73. Write the correct name next to the corresponding number on the map.

1.		9.	
2.		10.	
3.		11.	
4.		12.	
5.		13.	
6.		14.	
7.		15.	
8.			

2. According to the map, what are the two main uses of land in the Great Lakes basin?

_____

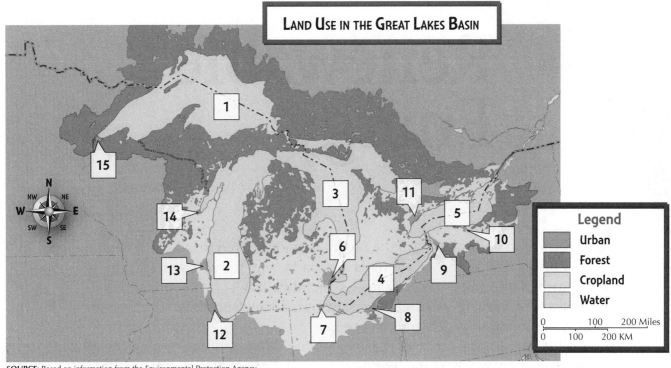

LAND USE IN THE GREAT LAKES BASIN

1

15

N
NW   NE
W   E
SW   SE
S

14

13   2

12

3

6

4

7

11

5

10

9

8

Legend
Urban
Forest
Cropland
Water

0   100   200 Miles
0   100   200 KM

SOURCE: Based on information from the Environmental Protection Agency

3. Based on the map, which two Great Lakes appear to have the most urban areas? Which two lakes have the least?

_____

_____

_____

4. Based on your reading of this lesson, name one way urban growth has affected land use in the Great Lakes basin.

_____

_____

_____

Refer to the information on Appendix page 103 to answer questions 5, 6, and 7.

5. Which is the deepest Great Lake? Which is the shallowest?

_____

6. Which Great Lake has the longest shoreline?

_____

7. Which Great Lake lies entirely within the U.S.?

_____

Renewable Energy

Coal, oil, and natural gas are the most commonly used fossil fuels in the United States. **Fossil fuels** are made from the remains of decayed plants and animals. They use combustion—the process of burning—to create energy. Fossil fuels supply about 85 percent of the energy we use in the United States. The costs of these resources will increase as the world supply is diminished over time. Fossil fuels are limited resources. One day, the supply will run out.

Nuclear energy is another source of electrical power. A nuclear power plant uses uranium, a mineral from Earth, in a process that creates heat. This heat powers **turbines,** machines with blades like a fan, to create electricity. There is a fear of nuclear power because the radioactive waste it generates is dangerous.

Renewable energy sources, such as wind power, hydropower, and solar power, will never be used up. With **wind power,** the wind turns a turbine's blades, which spin a shaft connected to a generator. **Hydropower** plants capture flowing water and move it through turbines. With **solar power,** panels use mirrors to concentrate and capture the sun's heat to run conventional generators. All of these renewable energy sources create electricity.

Hydropower plants capture the energy in flowing water and convert it to electricity.

Solar power panels capture the sun's heat and convert it to electricity.

Renewable Energy	Positives	Negatives
Wind Power	Renewable, clean fuel source; produces no air pollution; low cost; creates income for rural land owners	Large up-front investment; wind may be inconsistent; good wind sites often far from cities; some objections to noise of rotors and overall appearance
Hydropower	Renewable, clean fuel source; produces no air pollution	May limit the passage of migrating fish; lower water quality; alters stream levels; changes natural habitat; can be undependable in times of drought
Solar Power	Renewable, clean fuel source; produces no air pollution; low cost	More practical in southern states than in northern climates
Fossil Fuels		
Coal	Makes affordable electricity; can be mined throughout many areas of the United States; already compatible with most power stations; may be used in the future to make clean-burning fuels for transportation	Coal-fired power plants create great amounts of air and water pollution; strip mining for coal can damage the environment.
Oil (Petroleum)	Products made from crude oil, such as gasoline, diesel fuel, and home heating oil, are commonly available through the U.S. fuel supply network	Prices vary widely; over time, world supply will be diminished and prices will increase; fuels made from crude oil produce air pollution; dependence upon foreign supplies can create national security issues
Natural Gas	Easy to transport in pipelines; produces less air pollution than other fossil fuels	Prices vary widely; over time, world supply will be diminished and prices will increase; dependence upon foreign supplies can create national security issues
Nuclear Fuel		
Uranium	Fairly inexpensive; does not pollute the air; can produce a large amount of energy from very small amounts of fuel.	Though unlikely, the result of a plant malfunction could be the contamination of a wide area; radioactive waste products are very dangerous and require special handling.

Build Your
Map Skills

Read a Wind Power Map

Wind power has enormous potential as an alternative energy source. It is a renewable, clean fuel source. It produces no air pollution, it can be generated at a relatively low cost, and creates income for rural land owners when wind farms (groups of wind turbines) are built on their property.

However, wind power does have its limitations. Though they can generate electricity cheaply, the construction and placement of wind turbines requires a large investment. In addition, wind may be inconsistent, and good sites often lie far from the cities that consume the most electricity. People living near wind farms may also object to their noise and overall appearance.

Wind is created by the sun warming Earth, so wind is really a type of solar energy. A turbine is a mechanical way of taking energy from the wind and converting it into electricity. The wind turns the turbine's blades, which spin a shaft; the shaft is connected to a generator that makes electricity.

Wind power is not a realistic alternative energy source everywhere in the United States. For this reason, the Department of Energy has created a national wind atlas to show how practical wind power might be in specific areas.

Wind resources are classified by wind power density, a measurement of how much energy is available at a particular site for conversion by a turbine. Seven different wind classes have been established, with higher classes corresponding to higher wind power. Generally, electricity can be produced from wind in areas with wind classes of 3 and above, though classes 4–7 are the best match for today's technology.

In the right areas of the country, wind farms can generate electricity.

Refer to the map and answer the following questions.

1. Generally describe the parts of the United States that have the best potential for using wind power to generate electricity.

   _____

   _____

   _____

2. Which parts of the country appear to have the least potential for using wind power to generate electricity?

   _____

   _____

3. According to the map, what wind power class is your part of the country?

   _____

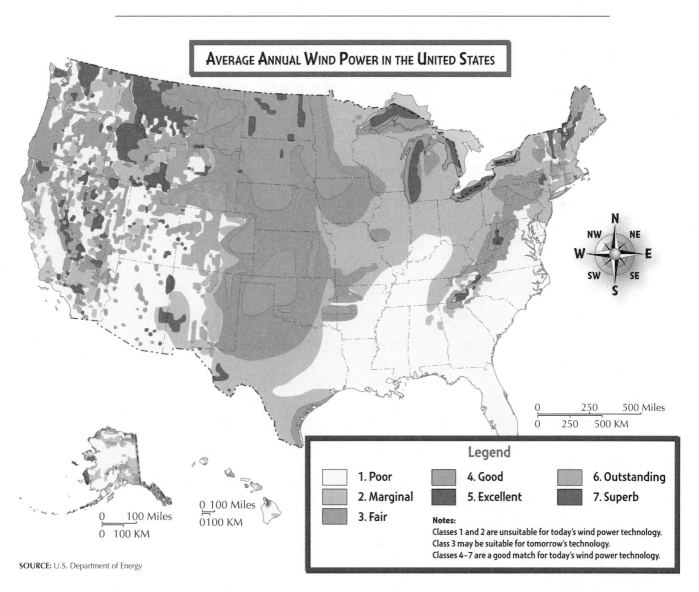

AVERAGE ANNUAL WIND POWER IN THE UNITED STATES

0   250   500 Miles
0   250   500 KM

0   100 Miles
0   100 KM

0   100 Miles
0   100 KM

Legend

	1. Poor		4. Good		6. Outstanding
	2. Marginal		5. Excellent		7. Superb
	3. Fair				

Notes:
Classes 1 and 2 are unsuitable for today's wind power technology.
Class 3 may be suitable for tomorrow's technology.
Classes 4–7 are a good match for today's wind power technology.

SOURCE: U.S. Department of Energy

LESSON 13

Do a Home Energy Audit

Why is it important to use energy wisely?

To be a responsible energy consumer, you need to understand how the energy you use every day is created. You should also know how much energy you use every day and learn about ways you might use less. Review the information on pages 73–75 and then answer questions 1–3.

1. What do you think is the greatest problem with our nation's dependence on fossil fuels?

   _____

2. What is a turbine? How is it used to make electricity?

   _____

   _____

   _____

   _____

3. What do nuclear power plants use to generate electricity? Why do some people fear nuclear power?

   _____

   _____

   _____

   The chart on the next page shows the many ways electricity is generated in the United States. Use the chart to answer questions 4 and 5.

4. According to the chart, what is the source of most of the electricity produced in the United States?

   _____

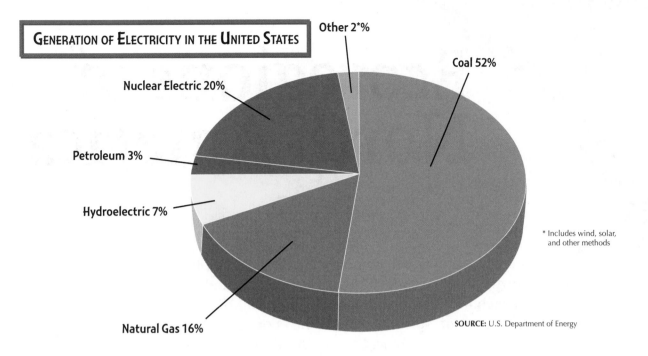

GENERATION OF ELECTRICITY IN THE UNITED STATES

Other 2*%

Coal 52%

Nuclear Electric 20%

Petroleum 3%

Hydroelectric 7%

Natural Gas 16%

* Includes wind, solar, and other methods

SOURCE: U.S. Department of Energy

5. How much of the electricity generated in the United States is produced by nuclear energy? How much is produced as hydroelectric power?

_____

Through a home energy audit, you can determine how much energy your home consumes and find ways to make your home more energy efficient. An energy audit will show you problems that can be fixed to save your family money and to conserve energy. Perform a simple home energy audit by answering the following questions on a separate piece of paper.

6. How is your home heated? For example, do you use natural gas or heating oil? How old is your home's heating and cooling equipment? Units more than 15 years old may not be energy efficient.

7. Go through your home looking for air leaks (drafts). Possible sources include electrical outlets, along baseboards, and around windows and doors. List any you find.

8. Examine the wattage size of light bulbs in your home. Could you use lower-watt bulbs or fluorescent bulbs in some lamps? Write down this information.

9. Outside your home, look for cracks and holes in the building's mortar, foundation, and siding. Any openings you find should be sealed appropriately.

10. Your home's attic could be a great source of heat loss if it is not insulated. Your water heater, hot water pipes, and furnace ducts should all be insulated as well. Write down any areas that need improvement.

Ecoregions of North America

Scientists who study Earth sometimes organize the planet into zones according to the types of **organisms** (plants and animals) that live in each area and the kind of weather that occurs there. One common division scientists use is the ecoregion. The word *ecoregion* is short for *ecological region.* An **ecoregion** can be described as an area of land or water that has a collection of plants and animals that is unique to that area. These plants and animals are dependent upon one another for their survival.

Terrestrial ecoregions are those regions that are on land. A desert is an example of a terrestrial ecoregion. **Aquatic ecoregions** are those regions that are in water. Lakes and **wetlands** are examples of aquatic ecoregions. Appendix pages 104–105 describe many common **landforms** and **water forms** that can be found in various ecoregions.

The types of plants that can live in an ecoregion are determined by climate. **Climate** is the usual pattern of weather in a particular place, including **precipitation. Elevation** (height in relation to sea level) and soil type also affect the types of plants that can grow in an ecoregion. The types of plants in an ecoregion determine the kind of animals that can live there. Ecoregions are roughly related to the lines of latitude, another indication that they are linked to climate. (See Appendix page 97 to learn more about latitude and longitude.)

Altitude affects the types of plants that can grow in an ecoregion.

Ecoregions help scientists and government leaders develop conservation plans that help to maintain biodiversity in an area. The term *biodiversity* (or biological diversity) refers to the variety of plant and animal species living in a certain area. A conservation plan helps to preserve **habitat,** or the places where plants and animals live. A conservation plan helps to identify animals and plants that may become endangered and helps to ensure that these organisms are not destroyed.

Some ecoregions are threatened by nonnative or **invasive species.** These are types of plants or animals that have been introduced to an area where they do not occur naturally. They may eventually displace or destroy the native organisms of an ecoregion. Examples of invasive insects include the emerald ash borer and gypsy moth. A plant called *kudzu* is another example.

Invasive species not only can threaten an ecoregion's biodiversity, but they can also have an economic impact. For example, the Asian longhorned beetle was accidentally introduced into the United States about 10 years ago. It is expected to infect and damage millions of acres of hardwood trees. This could have an effect upon the lumber industry by increasing prices of certain types of wood.

Wetlands are also called aquatic ecoregions.

Asian Longhorned Beetle

Boxelder tree killed by the Asian Longhorned Beetle

Build Your

Map Skills

Understanding Ecoregions

Temperate ecoregions generally lie at mid-latitude. They usually do not experience the temperature extremes of northern or southern latitudes. Many types of **deciduous trees** are found in temperate ecoregions. Deciduous trees, such as maple trees, produce leaves, which usually drop every fall.

North of the temperate ecoregions, **coniferous trees** become more common. Coniferous trees, such as spruce and pine trees, produce needles rather than leaves. Ecoregions of the extreme northern latitudes have no trees at all. **Tropical ecoregions** are warm and usually humid. These areas lie close to the equator. Grasslands or forests predominate there, depending on rainfall amounts.

Appendix pages 104–105 describe the ecoregion types shown on the map on the next page. Use the appendix and the map on the next page to answer the following questions.

1. Use the compass rose to describe where in the United States a marine west coast forests ecoregion can be found.

   _____

   _____

   _____

2. Name and describe the ecoregion along most of the Atlantic coast of the United States.

   _____

   _____

   _____

   _____

   _____

3. Where would you need to travel in the United States if you wanted to visit a tropical wet forest?

_____

4. What is the name of the northernmost ecoregion in which trees can grow? Can this ecoregion be found anywhere in the United States?

_____

_____

5. Name three ecoregions that lie north of 60°N latitude. Which two ecoregions occupy the smallest area north of this line?

_____

_____

_____

6. Name the two ecoregions that occupy the most area between 30°N and 40°N latitude.

_____

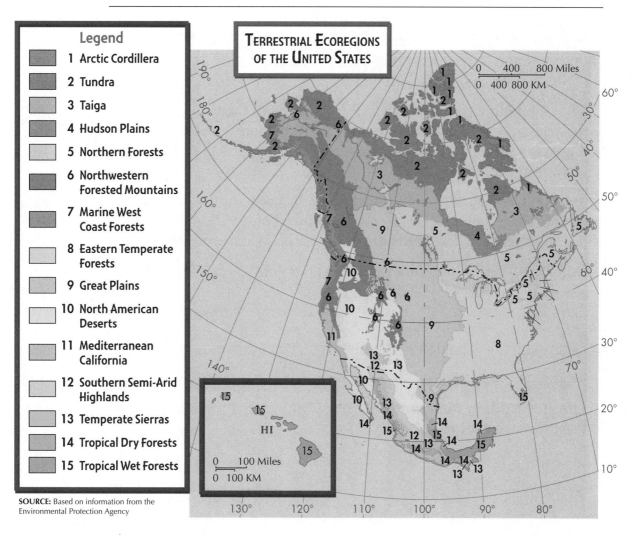

Legend
1 Arctic Cordillera
2 Tundra
3 Taiga
4 Hudson Plains
5 Northern Forests
6 Northwestern Forested Mountains
7 Marine West Coast Forests
8 Eastern Temperate Forests
9 Great Plains
10 North American Deserts
11 Mediterranean California
12 Southern Semi-Arid Highlands
13 Temperate Sierras
14 Tropical Dry Forests
15 Tropical Wet Forests

TERRESTRIAL ECOREGIONS OF THE UNITED STATES

SOURCE: Based on information from the Environmental Protection Agency

LESSON 14

Be a Naturalist

Why is it important to understand the environment you live in?

Have you ever gone bird-watching or waded through a creek looking for frogs? Do you like to study ants as they march back and forth from their anthills? Then maybe you're a budding naturalist! A **naturalist** is someone who studies nature, usually in the field (outdoors) rather than in a laboratory.

In this activity, you will take on the role of a naturalist. You will study the landforms and water forms that are in your ecoregion. You will learn about some plants and animals that make their homes there, too.

Try to get out into nature to answer as many of these questions as you can, just like a real naturalist would do. Visit some nearby parks or nature areas. You might be able to answer some questions just by walking around your neighborhood.

You can use resources from this lesson, from the Appendix, and from the library to help answer some questions. Before you begin, use the map on page 83 to determine the ecoregion in which you live.

1. Determine the temperature ranges in your ecoregion for the four seasons.

   _____

2. Determine the elevation of the place you live in relation to sea level.

   _____

3. List at least three landforms that occur in your ecoregion. Also list at least three water forms.

   _____

   _____

4. List five plants that are native to your ecoregion. At least two of those plants should be trees.

_____

_____

_____

5. List five animals that are native to your ecoregion. At least two of those animals should be birds.

_____

_____

_____

6. Are any landforms, water forms, plants, or animals in your ecoregion threatened by urban sprawl? (**Urban sprawl** is the uncontrolled or unplanned growth of urban areas into the countryside.)

_____

_____

_____

7. Read the local newspaper and listen to the news. Are people being affected by pollution in your area? What are the pollution issues in your community?

_____

_____

_____

8. Are invasive species a problem in your ecoregion? If so, describe them.

_____

_____

_____

9. Make a list of the conservation efforts that are being made in your ecoregion to help preserve natural areas or correct pollution problems. List the names of some of the groups and organizations that are trying to help.

_____

_____

_____

Election Geography

In Lesson 2, pages 12–13, you learned about the U.S. Census Bureau and how the census is conducted every 10 years. In this lesson, you will learn more about how the census can affect the way our nation is governed.

There are two legislative groups in the U.S. government: the Senate and the House of Representatives. Together, they make the laws that govern the nation. Regardless of population, every state has two senators who are elected every six years. However, the number of representatives each state has in the House is decided by its population. Due to shifts in population, a state could gain representation, called a *seat,* in the House or it could lose a seat. There are 435 seats in the House, and every state is guaranteed at least one representative. Elections for the House of Representatives take place every two years.

What does this mean to you? If your state gains a seat in the House, it will have a greater say in making the laws and governing the nation. But if your state loses a House seat, the people from your state will have less of a voice in how the nation is governed. This process of adjusting congressional representation every 10 years based on population changes is called **reapportionment.**

The number of representatives from your state could also affect a presidential election. Every four years, the people in your state cast their votes for president. In most states, the presidential candidate who gets the most votes wins all the state's electoral votes. **Electoral votes** are cast by **electors,** or members of the Electoral College. The number of electors is determined by adding the number of a state's senators to the number of its representatives. Vermont has 1 representative and 2 senators, for example, so it gets 3 electoral votes during a presidential election.

There are 538 members of the Electoral College: 100 electors (one for each U.S. senator); 435 electors (one for each House member); plus 3 from the District of Columbia, where the federal government is located.

Map 1 shows how the 2000 census changed the number of representatives that each state gets in the U.S. House of Representatives. (See Appendix page 106 for a key to state abbreviations.) Because the census is conducted every 10 years, the map compares the distribution of representatives based on the 2000 census with that based on the 1990 census. For example, as you can see on the map, Connecticut has 5 representatives. Connecticut lost one seat in the House in 2000, compared with the number it had in 1990. To figure the number of electoral votes for each state, add 2 (for 2 senators) to the number for each state on the map. So, Connecticut has 7 electoral votes.

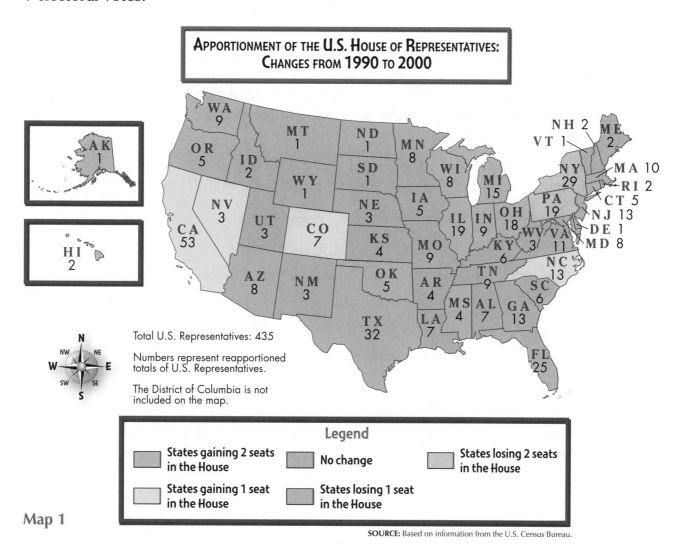

APPORTIONMENT OF THE **U.S. HOUSE OF REPRESENTATIVES:** CHANGES FROM **1990** TO **2000**

Total U.S. Representatives: 435

Numbers represent reapportioned totals of U.S. Representatives.

The District of Columbia is not included on the map.

Legend

States gaining 2 seats in the House

No change

States losing 2 seats in the House

States gaining 1 seat in the House

States losing 1 seat in the House

Map 1

SOURCE: Based on information from the U.S. Census Bureau.

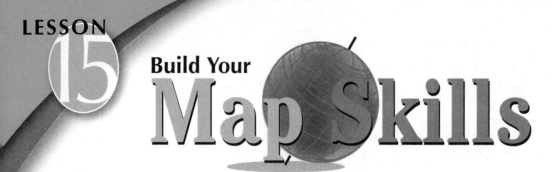

Build Your Map Skills

Read an Election Map

Much has been made of the geography of the 2004 presidential election between George W. Bush and John Kerry. This was the first election with an electoral college based on the 2000 census. Geography became important because it appeared as though people voted for the Democratic or Republican candidates based on where they lived. In addition, each party won most of the same states in 2004 as in the election of 2000.

Use Map 1 on page 87 to determine which states gained and lost electoral votes in the 2000 census (and the 2004 election) due to reapportionment. (Do not include the District of Columbia.) Record your findings on a separate piece of paper. Then refer to Maps 2 and 3, and answer the following questions.

1. Which states gaining electoral votes in the 2000 census voted Republican in the 2004 election? Which voted Democratic?

   _____

   _____

2. Which states losing electoral votes in 2004 voted Republican? Which voted Democratic?

   _____

   _____

   _____

3. Did any states vote for the Democratic candidate in 2000 but the Republican candidate in 2004? Which states went Republican in 2000 but Democratic in 2004?

   _____

   _____

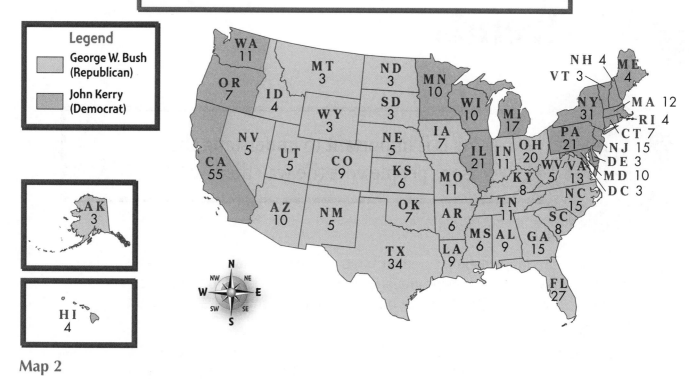

PRESIDENTIAL ELECTION OF 2004
NUMBER OF ELECTORAL VOTES FOR EACH STATE AND THE DISTRICT OF COLUMBIA

Legend
George W. Bush (Republican)
John Kerry (Democrat)

WA 11
OR 7
ID 4
MT 3
ND 3
MN 10
WI 10
MI 17
NH 4
VT 3
ME 4
NY 31
MA 12
RI 4
CT 7
NV 5
UT 5
WY 3
SD 3
NE 5
IA 7
IL 21
IN 11
OH 20
PA 21
NJ 15
DE 3
MD 10
DC 3
CA 55
CO 9
KS 6
MO 11
KY 8
WV 5
VA 13
AZ 10
NM 5
OK 7
AR 6
TN 11
NC 15
SC 8
MS 6
AL 9
GA 15
TX 34
LA 9
FL 27

AK 3
HI 4

Map 2

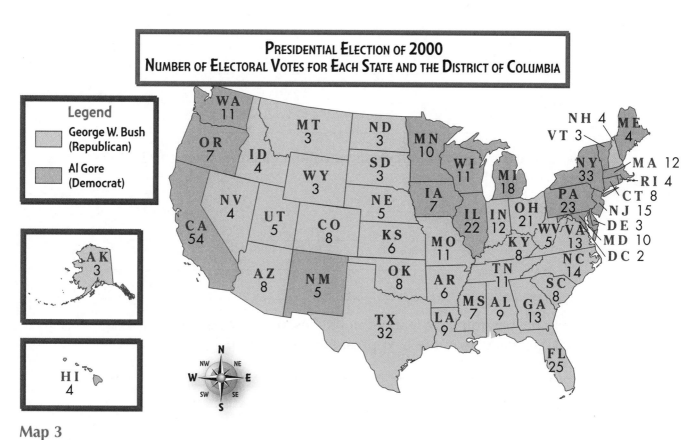

PRESIDENTIAL ELECTION OF 2000
NUMBER OF ELECTORAL VOTES FOR EACH STATE AND THE DISTRICT OF COLUMBIA

Legend
George W. Bush (Republican)
Al Gore (Democrat)

WA 11
OR 7
ID 4
MT 3
ND 3
MN 10
WI 11
MI 18
NH 4
VT 3
ME 4
NY 33
MA 12
RI 4
CT 8
NV 4
UT 5
WY 3
SD 3
NE 5
IA 7
IL 22
IN 12
OH 21
PA 23
NJ 15
DE 3
MD 10
DC 2
CA 54
CO 8
KS 6
MO 11
KY 8
WV 5
VA 13
AZ 8
NM 5
OK 8
AR 6
TN 11
NC 14
SC 8
MS 7
AL 9
GA 13
TX 32
LA 9
FL 25

AK 3
HI 4

Map 3

Understand Voting Trends

Something to **Think** About

Why is it important to understand the reasons people vote the way they do?

Compare Maps 4–6 on the next page with Maps 2 and 3 on page 89, and then answer the following questions. (Note that the "Independent" candidates on Maps 5 and 6 were both Democrats running for president under a third party.)

1. Which parts of the country tended to vote for Democratic (and Independent) candidates in the 1950s and 1960s? Did this change by the 2000 and 2004 elections? Explain.

_____

_____

_____

_____

_____

2. Have any areas of the country gained or lost electors since the 1950s? If so, describe this change.

_____

_____

_____

_____

3. Based on what you have learned in this lesson, how do you think your state will vote in the next presidential election?

_____

_____

_____

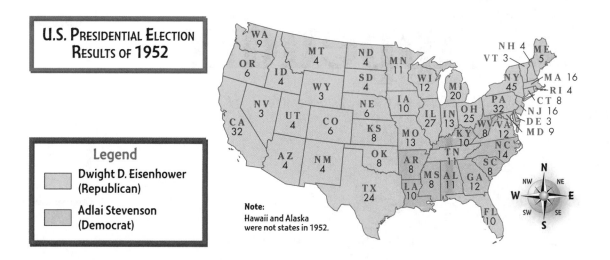

Map 4

U.S. PRESIDENTIAL ELECTION RESULTS OF 1952

Legend
- Dwight D. Eisenhower (Republican)
- Adlai Stevenson (Democrat)

Note:
Hawaii and Alaska were not states in 1952.

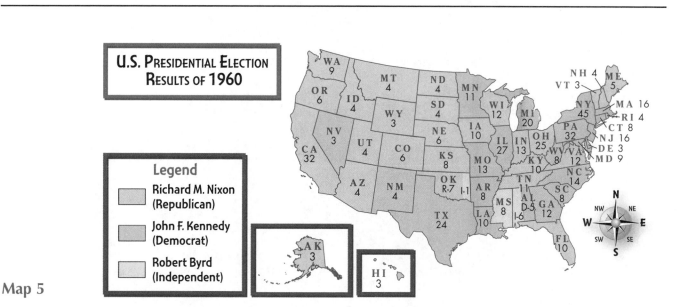

Map 5

U.S. PRESIDENTIAL ELECTION RESULTS OF 1960

Legend
- Richard M. Nixon (Republican)
- John F. Kennedy (Democrat)
- Robert Byrd (Independent)

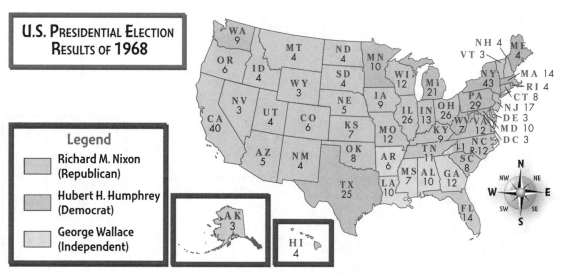

Map 6

U.S. PRESIDENTIAL ELECTION RESULTS OF 1968

Legend
- Richard M. Nixon (Republican)
- Hubert H. Humphrey (Democrat)
- George Wallace (Independent)

Appendix

Legend

⊛ National Capital
★ State Capital
• Major City
— International boundary
----- State boundary

THE UNITED STATES

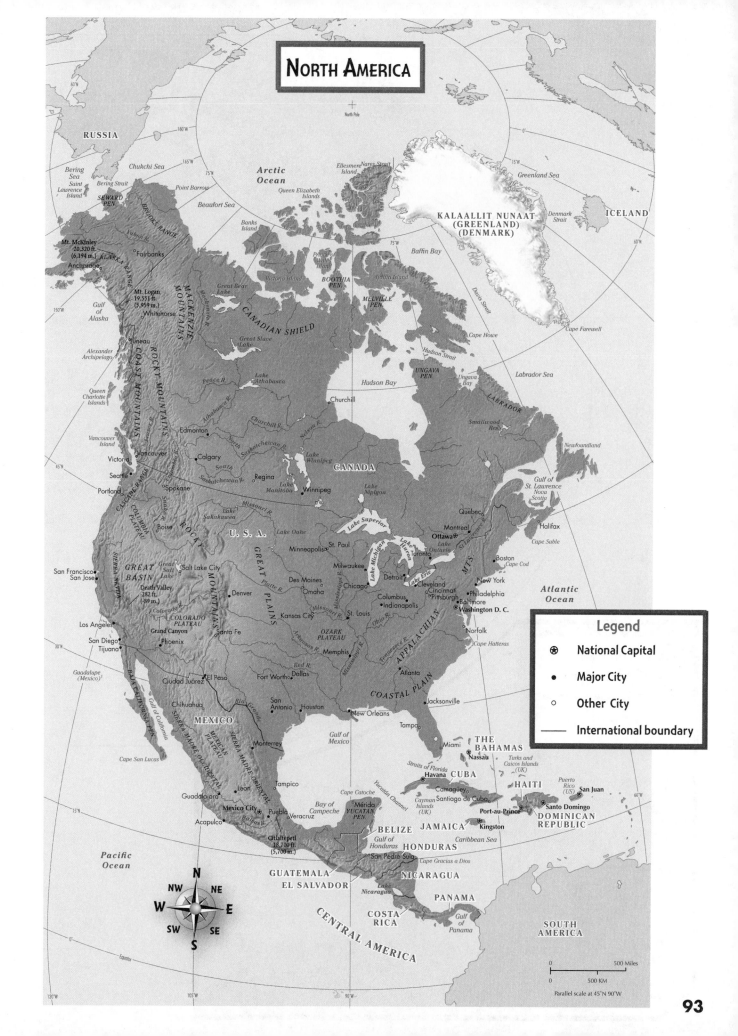

NORTH AMERICA

RUSSIA

Bering
Sea
Saint
Lawrence
Island

Chukchi Sea

Arctic
Ocean

North Pole

Ellesmere
Island

Nares Strait

Greenland Sea

ICELAND

Point Barrow

Beaufort Sea

Queen Elizabeth
Islands

KALAALLIT NUNAAT
(GREENLAND)
(DENMARK)

Denmark
Strait

SEWARD
PEN.

Bering Strait

BROOKS RANGE

Banks
Island

Baffin Bay

ALASKA RANGE

Fairbanks

Mt. McKinley
20,320 ft.
(6,194 m.)

Anchorage

Victoria Island

Prince of
Wales
Island

BOOTHIA
PEN.

Baffin Island

75°W

Cape Howe

Cape Farewell

Mt. Logan
19,551 ft.
(5,959 m.)

Whitehorse

Gulf
of
Alaska

Great Bear
Lake

MELVILLE
PEN.

Davis Strait

Juneau

MACKENZIE MOUNTAINS

CANADIAN SHIELD

Hudson Strait

Alexander
Archipelago

Great Slave
Lake

UNGAVA
PEN.

Labrador Sea

ROCKY MOUNTAINS

COAST MOUNTAINS

Peace R.

Mackenzie R.

Ungava
Bay

LABRADOR

Queen
Charlotte
Islands

Lake
Athabasca

Hudson Bay

Smallwood
Res.

Vancouver
Island

Athabasca R.

Churchill R.

Churchill

Newfoundland

Edmonton

North Saskatchewan R.

Nelson R.

Victoria

Calgary

Lake
Winnipeg

CANADA

Gulf of
St. Lawrence
Nova
Scotia

Vancouver

South Saskatchewan R.

Regina

Seattle

Spokane

Winnipeg

Lake
Manitoba

Lake
Nipigon

Quebec

Halifax

Portland

CASCADE RANGE

COLUMBIA
PLATEAU

Snake R.

Columbia R.

Lake Superior

Montreal

Ottawa

Cape Sable

Boise

ROCKY

Lake
Sakakawea

Missouri R.

U.S.A.

Lake Oahe

Minneapolis

St. Paul

Lake Michigan

Lake Huron

Toronto

Lake
Ontario

St. Lawrence R.

Boston

Cape Cod

San Francisco

San Jose

GREAT
BASIN

Great
Salt
Lake

Salt Lake City

MOUNTAINS

GREAT PLAINS

Des Moines

Milwaukee

Chicago

Detroit

Lake Erie

Cleveland

New York

SIERRA NEVADA

Death Valley
-282 ft.
(-86 m.)

Denver

Platte R.

Omaha

Cincinnati

Pittsburgh

Philadelphia

Atlantic
Ocean

COLORADO
PLATEAU

Colorado R.

Kansas City

Columbus

Indianapolis

St. Louis

Ohio R.

Baltimore

Washington D.C.

Los Angeles

Grand Canyon

Santa Fe

OZARK
PLATEAU

Arkansas R.

Mississippi R.

APPALACHIAN MTS.

Norfolk

San Diego

Phoenix

Memphis

Tennessee R.

Cape Hatteras

Tijuana

Guadalupe
(Mexico)

Ciudad Juárez

El Paso

Red R.

Fort Worth

Dallas

Atlanta

COASTAL PLAIN

BAJA CALIFORNIA PEN.

Chihuahua

Rio Grande

San
Antonio

Houston

Jacksonville

SIERRA MADRE OCCIDENTAL

MEXICO

MEXICAN
PLATEAU

New Orleans

Tampa

Miami

THE
BAHAMAS

Monterrey

Gulf of
Mexico

Nassau

Turks and
Caicos Islands
(UK)

Cape San Lucas

SIERRA MADRE ORIENTAL

Tampico

Cape Catoche

Straits of Florida

Havana

CUBA

HAITI

Puerto
Rico
(US)

San Juan

Guadalajara

Leon

Yucatán Channel

Camagüey

Santiago de Cuba

Port-au-Prince

Santo Domingo

Mexico City

Puebla

Veracruz

Mérida

YUCATAN
PEN.

Cayman
Islands
(UK)

Kingston

DOMINICAN
REPUBLIC

Acapulco

Balsas R.

Bay of
Campeche

BELIZE

JAMAICA

Caribbean Sea

Citlaltepetl
18,700 ft.
(5,700 m.)

Gulf of
Honduras

HONDURAS

San Pedro Sula

Cape Gracias a Dios

GUATEMALA

EL SALVADOR

Lake
Nicaragua

NICARAGUA

PANAMA

Pacific
Ocean

COSTA
RICA

Gulf of
Panama

SOUTH
AMERICA

CENTRAL AMERICA

Equator

N
NW NE
W E
SW SE
S

Legend

⊛ National Capital

● Major City

○ Other City

— International boundary

0   500 Miles

0   500 KM

Parallel scale at 45°N 90°W

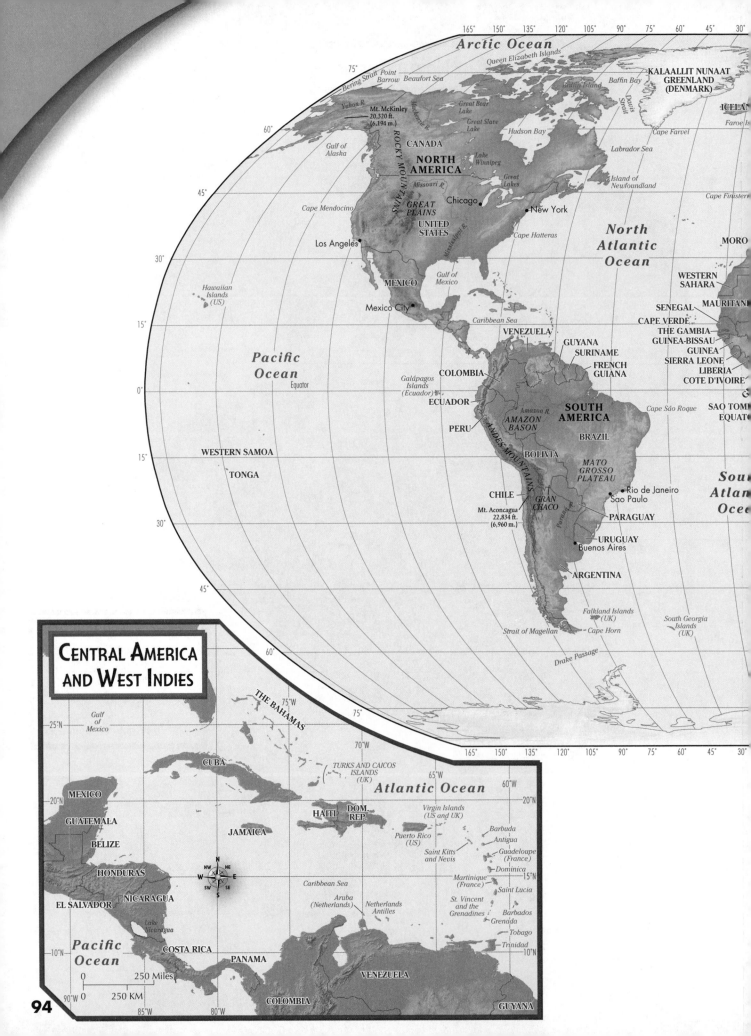

Arctic Ocean

75°

Queen Elizabeth Islands

Point Barrow

Bering Strait

Beaufort Sea

Baffin Island

Baffin Bay

Davis Strait

KALAALLIT NUNAAT GREENLAND (DENMARK)

ICELAN

Faroe Is

60°

Yukon R.

Mt. McKinley 20,320 ft. (6,194 m.)

Gulf of Alaska

Mackenzie R.

Great Bear Lake

Great Slave Lake

Hudson Bay

CANADA

ROCKY MOUNTAINS

NORTH AMERICA

Lake Winnipeg

Labrador Sea

Cape Farvel

45°

Cape Mendocino

GREAT PLAINS

Missouri R.

Chicago

Great Lakes

Island of Newfoundland

Cape Finisterr

North Atlantic Ocean

MORO

30°

Los Angeles

UNITED STATES

Mississippi R.

New York

Cape Hatteras

WESTERN SAHARA

Hawaiian Islands (US)

MEXICO

Gulf of Mexico

SENEGAL

MAURITANI

Mexico City

Caribbean Sea

CAPE VERDE

15°

Pacific Ocean

VENEZUELA

GUYANA SURINAME FRENCH GUIANA

THE GAMBIA GUINEA-BISSAU GUINEA SIERRA LEONE LIBERIA COTE D'IVOIRE

Equator

Galápagos Islands (Ecuador)

COLOMBIA

0°

ECUADOR

Amazon R.

AMAZON BASON

SOUTH AMERICA

Cape São Roque

SAO TOMM EQUATO

PERU

ANDES MOUNTAINS

BRAZIL

15°

WESTERN SAMOA

BOLIVIA

MATO GROSSO PLATEAU

Sou Atlan Oce

TONGA

CHILE

GRAN CHACO

Rio de Janeiro Sao Paulo

Mt. Aconcagua 22,834 ft. (6,960 m.)

Paraná R.

PARAGUAY

30°

URUGUAY Buenos Aires

ARGENTINA

45°

Falkland Islands (UK)

South Georgia Islands (UK)

Strait of Magellan

Cape Horn

60°

Drake Passage

165° 150° 135° 120° 105° 90° 75° 60° 45° 30°

CENTRAL AMERICA AND WEST INDIES

THE BAHAMAS

75°W

75°

25°N

Gulf of Mexico

70°W

65°W

60°W

CUBA

TURKS AND CAICOS ISLANDS (UK)

Atlantic Ocean

MEXICO

20°N

HAITI

DOM. REP.

Virgin Islands (US and UK)

20°N

GUATEMALA

JAMAICA

Puerto Rico (US)

Barbuda

Antigua

BELIZE

Saint Kitts and Nevis

Guadeloupe (France)

HONDURAS

Dominica

15°N

Martinique (France)

Saint Lucia

EL SALVADOR

NICARAGUA

Caribbean Sea

Aruba (Netherlands)

Netherlands Antilles

St. Vincent and the Grenadines

Barbados

Grenada

Lake Nicaragua

Tobago

Pacific Ocean

COSTA RICA

PANAMA

Trinidad

10°N

0   250 Miles

COLOMBIA

VENEZUELA

GUYANA

90°W   0   250 KM

85°W

80°W

94

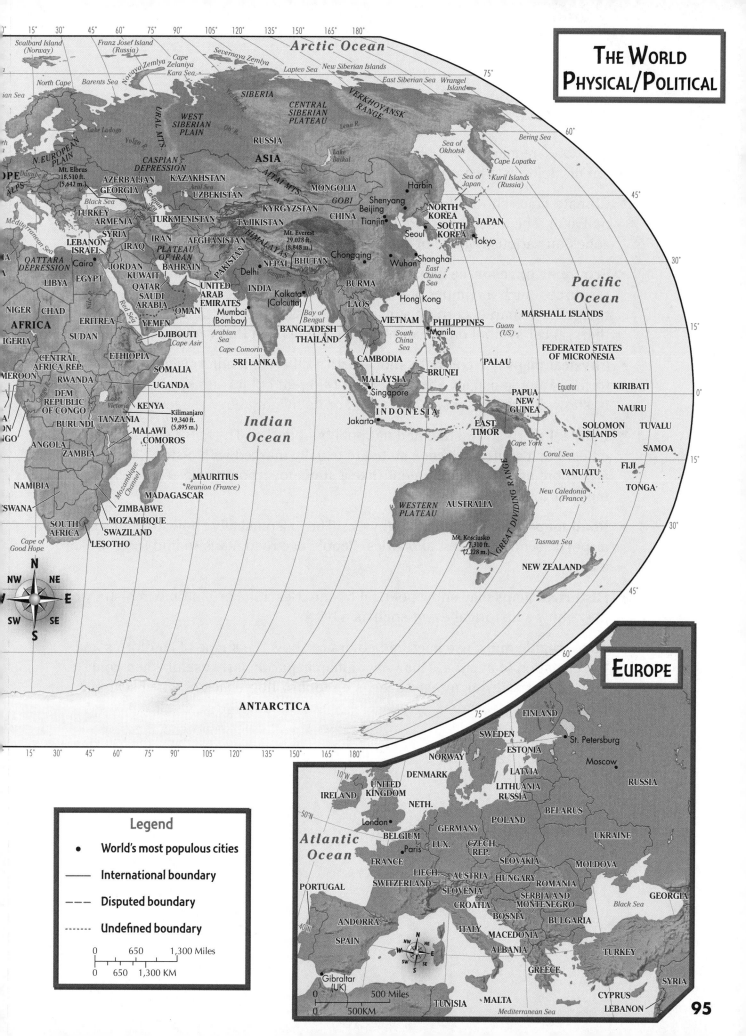

Arctic Ocean

Svalbard Island (Norway)
Franz Josef Island (Russia)
North Cape
Novaya Zemlya
Cape Zelaniya
Severnaya Zemlya
Laptev Sea
New Siberian Islands
East Siberian Sea
Wrangel Island

Barents Sea
Kara Sea
SIBERIA
CENTRAL SIBERIAN PLATEAU
VERKHOYANSK RANGE

ian Sea
Lake Ladoga
URAL MTS.
WEST SIBERIAN PLAIN
Ob R.
Victoria R.

N. EUROPEAN PLAIN
RUSSIA
ASIA
Lake Baikal
Bering Sea

OPE
ALPS
Mt. Elbrus 18,510 ft. (5,642 m.)
AZERBAIJAN
GEORGIA
CASPIAN DEPRESSION
Volga R.
KAZAKHSTAN
Aral Sea
UZBEKISTAN
ALTAI MTS.
MONGOLIA
GOBI
Harbin
Shenyang
NORTH KOREA
SOUTH KOREA
JAPAN
Cape Lopatka
Sea of Okhotsk
Kuril Islands (Russia)
Sea of Japan

Black Sea
TURKEY
ARMENIA
SYRIA
TURKMENISTAN
KYRGYZSTAN
TAJIKISTAN
CHINA
Beijing
Tianjin
Seoul
Tokyo

Mediterranean Sea
LEBANON
ISRAEL
IRAN
AFGHANISTAN
HIMALAYAS
Mt. Everest 29,028 ft. (8,848 m.)
NEPAL
BHUTAN
Chongqing
Wuhan
Shanghai
East China Sea

QATTARA DEPRESSION
Cairo
JORDAN
IRAQ
PLATEAU OF IRAN
BAHRAIN
PAKISTAN
Delhi
Ganges R.
BURMA
Hong Kong
Pacific Ocean

LIBYA
EGYPT
KUWAIT
QATAR
SAUDI ARABIA
UNITED ARAB EMIRATES
INDIA
Kolkata (Calcutta)
LAOS
MARSHALL ISLANDS

NIGER
CHAD
OMAN
YEMEN
Mumbai (Bombay)
Bay of Bengal
VIETNAM
PHILIPPINES
Manila
Guam (US)

AFRICA
ERITREA
DJIBOUTI
Arabian Sea
Cape Asir
BANGLADESH
THAILAND
South China Sea
FEDERATED STATES OF MICRONESIA

IGERIA
SUDAN
ETHIOPIA
Cape Comorin
SRI LANKA
CAMBODIA
PALAU

CENTRAL AFRICA REP.
RWANDA
SOMALIA
UGANDA
MALAYSIA
BRUNEI
Equator
KIRIBATI

MEROON
DEM. REPUBLIC OF CONGO
Lake Victoria
KENYA
Kilimanjaro 19,340 ft. (5,895 m.)
Singapore
INDONESIA
PAPUA NEW GUINEA
NAURU

A
ON
GO
BURUNDI
TANZANIA
MALAWI
COMOROS
Jakarta
EAST TIMOR
SOLOMON ISLANDS
TUVALU

ANGOLA
ZAMBIA
Indian Ocean
Cape York
Coral Sea
SAMOA

NAMIBIA
MAURITIUS
Reunion (France)
MADAGASCAR
VANUATU
New Caledonia (France)
FIJI
TONGA

SWANA
ZIMBABWE
MOZAMBIQUE
SWAZILAND
WESTERN PLATEAU
AUSTRALIA
GREAT DIVIDING RANGE

SOUTH AFRICA
LESOTHO
Cape of Good Hope
Mt. Kosciusko 7,310 ft. (2,228 m.)
Tasman Sea

NEW ZEALAND

Mozambique Channel

ANTARCTICA

N NE NW
W E
SW SE
S

Arctic Ocean coordinates: 75°, 60°, 45°, 30°, 15°, 0°, 15°, 30°, 45°, 60°, 75°

15° 30° 45° 60° 75° 90° 105° 120° 135° 150° 165° 180°

Legend

- **World's most populous cities**

— **International boundary**

- - - **Disputed boundary**

.... **Undefined boundary**

0   650   1,300 Miles
0   650   1,300 KM

FINLAND
SWEDEN
St. Petersburg
NORWAY
ESTONIA
Moscow
DENMARK
LATVIA
RUSSIA
IRELAND
UNITED KINGDOM
NETH.
LITHUANIA
RUSSIA
BELARUS
London
GERMANY
POLAND
UKRAINE
Atlantic Ocean
BELGIUM
LUX.
CZECH REP.
Paris
FRANCE
LIECH.
SLOVAKIA
MOLDOVA
SWITZERLAND
AUSTRIA
HUNGARY
ROMANIA
PORTUGAL
SLOVENIA
GEORGIA
CROATIA
SERBIA AND MONTENEGRO
Black Sea
ANDORRA
BOSNIA
BULGARIA
SPAIN
ITALY
MACEDONIA
ALBANIA
TURKEY
GREECE
Gibraltar (UK)
0   500 Miles
0   500KM
TUNISIA
MALTA
CYPRUS
LEBANON
SYRIA
Mediterranean Sea

10°W
50°N
40°N

N NE NW
W E
SW SE
S

95

Types of Maps

There are many types of maps. Each type of map shows something different. Below is a list of some of the most common types.

- **Climate maps** show information about the typical weather of a specific place on Earth. The different colors on a climate map show the different climate zones on various regions of Earth.

- **Economic or resource maps** use symbols to tell us what kinds of natural resources, such as timber or coal, an area has or what kind of work is done there. For example, corn on a map of Nebraska tells you that corn is grown there. A car symbol on a map of Michigan tells you that cars are built there.

- **Physical maps** use colors to show Earth's different landforms and water forms. Water is usually shown in blue. Different colors and symbols are used to show differences in land elevation, or its height above sea level.

- **Political maps** show state and national boundaries. They also show important cities. Capital cities within a state are usually marked with a star. Capital cities are where heads of government (like a state governor) and elected officials meet to govern.

- **Road maps** show roads and highways. They also usually show locations like airports, schools, parks, and cities. People use road maps to find their way on a trip.

- **Historical maps** may show political boundaries at a certain time in history or may show a historical event such as a battle.

- **Topographic maps** use lines and colors to show the shape of landforms and the elevation of an area. This type of map is particularly useful when going cross country through remote areas on foot or horseback or when searching remote areas by air.

Understanding Latitude and Longitude

The **equator** is an imaginary horizontal line drawn around the center of Earth. More lines are drawn parallel to the equator. These are called **lines (or parallels) of latitude.** The latitude of any place on Earth is its distance north or south of the equator, measured in degrees. The equator is 0°. The latitude of the North Pole is 90°N (this is read as "ninety degrees north"). The latitude of the South Pole is 90°S ("ninety degrees south").

The **prime meridian** is an imaginary vertical line around Earth from the North Pole to the South Pole. Other lines drawn parallel to the prime meridian are called **lines (or meridians) of longitude.** Like latitude, longitude is measured in degrees. The longitude of New York City, for example, is 74°W ("seventy-four degrees west").

The equator divides Earth into the northern and southern hemispheres. The prime meridian divides Earth into the western and eastern hemispheres. **Hemisphere** means *half of a globe.*

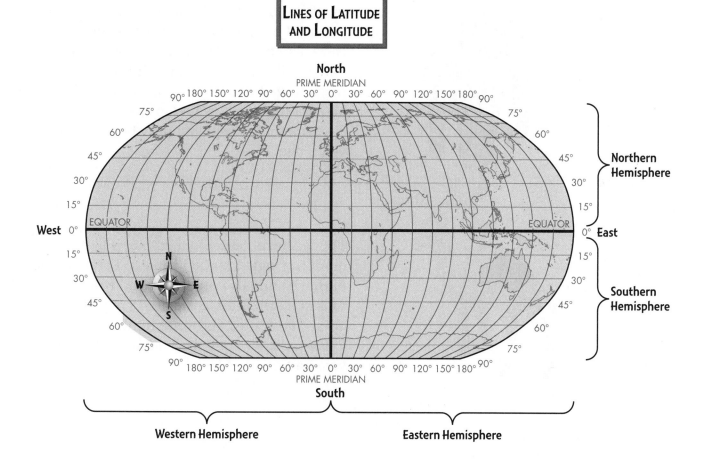

Extinct Animals of North America

Ice-age bison had long horns that were much longer than modern bison of the Great Plains. Unlike today's bison that live in grasslands, ice-age bison lived in woodland areas. This animal died out about 7,000 years ago, replaced by smaller bison.

Columbian mammoths had long, curved tusks and thick hair. The largest of these animals were 14 feet tall and weighed as much as four tons. Mammoths ate several hundred pounds of vegetation daily. They were also hunted for food by Paleo-Indians. Paleo-Indians used mammoth bones and tusks to make tools and carvings. Mammoths could not adapt to the warming environment. They died out about 11,000 years ago.

The **western camel** looked much like modern single-humped camels. Large herds of these animals could be found from Alaska all the way to Mexico. They ate grass and leaves and were hunted by Paleo-Indians. They died out about 10,000 years ago.

The **giant short-faced bear** was a feared predator that fed on bison, horses, and deer. They lived in the grasslands of western North America, from Alaska to Mexico. This bear died out about 10,000 years ago.

Saber-toothed cats had long fangs that they used to tear the flesh of their prey. Adults weighed up to 450 pounds. They usually stalked and attacked their prey from hiding places. Saber-toothed cats went extinct about 11,000 years ago.

The **giant beaver** could weigh up to 450 pounds, over four times as much as modern beavers. Giant beavers lived in lakes, ponds, and wetlands. They ate plants and trees. They could not build dams like today's beavers. They became extinct about 10,000 years ago when they lost much of their wetland habitat due to climate change. This beaver lived all over North America, but it was probably most common in the Midwest.

Jefferson's Ground Sloth was similar to modern sloths of South America. They were about 9 feet long and were covered with long hair. They lived all over eastern and western North America. This sloth fed on tree leaves and lived in the forest. It became extinct about 9,000 years ago.

Expeditions of Zebulon Pike

In 1805, Lieutenant Zebulon Pike was given an assignment from commanding General James Wilkinson. He was to explore the region of the upper Mississippi River and discover its source. He was also to purchase land from Native Americans for future military posts. Pike was to warn the British at various trading posts to leave U.S. soil.

Pike went up the Mississippi on a keelboat with 20 men. Unfortunately, he did not have an interpreter and had very little scientific equipment. Pike met with members of the Sioux nation and bought over 150,000 acres for military use. He made contact with the British at a number of their trading posts in the area and warned them to leave U.S. soil, though this had little effect. He was not able to locate the source of the Mississippi River.

Upon Pike's return in 1806, General Wilkinson ordered him to the disputed southwest border region of the Louisiana Purchase. He was to explore the headwaters of the Arkansas River and then move south and find the source of the Red River and follow it to the Mississippi. Pike was entering territory that was occupied and claimed by the Spanish. He was really serving as a spy to locate Spanish forts and determine their strength.

Pike and 23 men began their journey up the Missouri River in the summer of 1806. They were poorly prepared, having only summer clothing and no scientific instruments. His party explored both the Arkansas and Red rivers.

Pike and his party were captured by the Spanish. During his captivity, Pike was marched to Albuquerque, El Paso, and Chihuahua. Though Pike was not well educated, he took careful notes about the Spanish, the Native Americans, and his experiences while in captivity. He recorded much information about the culture, military outposts, and communities of New Spain. Pike and some of his men were eventually released in U.S. territory.

After his expedition into the southwest, Pike published *An Account of Expeditions to the Sources of the Mississippi and through the Western Parts of Louisiana* in 1810. The book provided Americans with a description of New Spain. His maps of the region were used for years. However, Pike and his men received no land or other compensation for their difficult expedition.

Lewis and Clark and the Corps of Discovery

President Thomas Jefferson's instructions to Lewis and Clark were as follows:

". . . Explore the Missouri river & such principal stream of it as by its course and communication with the waters of the Pacific Ocean . . . may offer the most direct & practicable water communication across this continent for the purpose of commerce. Take observations of latitude & longitude, courses of the river, variations of the compass; [Observe] the soil & face of the country, . . . growth & vegetable productions; the animals of the country, the mineral productions of every kind; volcanic appearances, . . . climate, . . . particular plants, birds, reptiles or insects."

Jefferson thought Meriwether Lewis would be a fine leader for the Corps of Discovery. Jefferson wrote:

"It was impossible to find a character who to a compleat science in botany, natural history, mineralogy & astronomy, joined the firmness of constitution & character, prudence, habits adapted to the woods, & a familiarity with the Indian manners & character, requisite for this undertaking. All the latter qualifications Capt. Lewis has."

The Corps of Discovery:

- provided the U.S. with knowledge of the American West through its detailed journals.
- encouraged trade in the West.
- observed and described 178 plants and 122 animals.
- proved that it was possible to successfully travel over land to the Pacific Ocean.
- established relations with Native Americans of the West and described their cultures.
- helped to excite the imagination of Americans in regard to the West

Among the many plants and animals discovered by the expedition were:

Black-tailed prairie dog	Wild alfalfa
Grizzly bear	Salt sage
Mule deer	Blue flax
Swift fox	Indian tobacco
Trumpeter swan	White milkwort
Black-billed magpie	Western hognose snake
Blue catfish	Western rattlesnake
Channel catfish	

Topics and People of the Civil War

The Fugitive Slave Act of 1850: This federal law passed by Congress in 1850 fined federal marshals $1,000 if they refused to arrest a runaway slave. People who helped slaves escape could also be fined and jailed.

The Underground Railroad: A network of secret routes operated before the Civil War by antislavery northerners that helped slaves escape to freedom.

The Emancipation Proclamation: An order issued by Abraham Lincoln on January 1, 1863, that freed most of the slaves in the United States.

The Thirteenth Amendment: This constitutional amendment was ratified on December 6, 1865. It outlawed all slavery in the United States.

Henry Clay (1777–1852): American congressman and senator known as the Great Compromiser for his ability to negotiate laws acceptable to both northern and southern statesmen regarding the issue of slavery.

John Brown (1800–1859): Abolitionist who supported and practiced violence against proslavery advocates. He launched an unsuccessful raid on a federal armory at Harper's Ferry, Virginia, in 1859 and was tried and executed.

Dred Scott (1795?–1858): A slave who unsuccessfully sued for his freedom in 1857 in the famous case *Dred Scott* v *Sandford*. His case resulted in the landmark U.S. Supreme Court ruling that slaves were property.

Robert E. Lee (1807–1870): Confederate general whose brilliant tactics against superior Union forces were widely admired. After the Civil War ended, he urged northerners and southerners to reunite.

Abraham Lincoln (1809–1865): American president during the Civil War who is widely regarded as one of the greatest presidents in American history for his efforts to preserve the Union.

Jefferson Davis (1808–1889): President of the Confederacy during the Civil War. His leadership during the war has been generally criticized by historians.

Harriet Tubman (1820?–1913): A former slave who escaped and became a conductor on the Underground Railroad, helping hundreds of slaves to freedom.

Fun Facts about the Great Lakes

Lake Superior

- This is the largest of the Great Lakes. It could hold all of the water in the other four Great Lakes, along with three more Lake Eries!
- Lake Superior is 600 feet above sea level. It is the highest of the Great Lakes.
- Lake Superior is the deepest Great Lake, too. It is as deep as 1,332 feet.
- Because Lake Superior is so deep, it's the coldest of the Great Lakes.

Lake Michigan

- Lake Michigan is the only Great Lake entirely within the United States. Each of the other Great Lakes is partly bordered by Canada.
- Lake Michigan is the second-largest of the Great Lakes in amount of water.
- Lake Michigan's shoreline has some of the world's largest freshwater sand dunes.
- Lake Michigan's greatest depth is 925 feet.

Lake Erie

- Lake Erie is the smallest of the Great Lakes in amount of water.
- Lake Erie's water levels change all the time. It gets water from lakes Superior, Huron, and Michigan.
- Lake Erie is the shallowest Great Lake. Its greatest depth is only about 210 feet.
- Lake Erie is the warmest of the Great Lakes.

Lake Ontario

- Lake Ontario is the smallest of the Great Lakes in area.
- Lake Ontario is the lowest of the Great Lakes. It is only about 243 feet above sea level.
- Boats could not pass from Lake Ontario into the other Great Lakes until locks were built to adjust the water level.
- Lake Ontario is connected to Lake Erie by the Niagara River. Niagara Falls is located where the two lakes meet.

Lake Huron

- Lake Huron has the longest shoreline of any of the Great Lakes.
- Lake Huron is the third-largest Great Lake in amount of water. It is the second-largest Great Lake in area.
- Lake Huron's greatest depth is 750 feet.

Ecoregions of North America

Arctic Cordillera	The climate in this region is cold, harsh, and dry. It has few plants and animals. Animals include Arctic hares and polar bears. Consists of rugged, ice-covered mountains. Most soils are frozen all year.
Tundra	This area lies between the arctic cordillera to the north and taiga to the south. Includes grasslands and mesas. Has short, cool summers and little precipitation. Wildlife includes caribou and moose. An important region for migratory birds.
Taiga	Short, cool summers and long, harsh winters. This region is known for its many thousands of lakes and vast wetlands. The taiga defines the northernmost area where trees can grow. It is home to many animals, such as moose and black bears. This is an important area for migratory birds.
Hudson Plains	This region consists of the wetlands along the southern portion of Hudson Bay. Vegetation consists of stunted forest and tundra. Animals include caribou, deer, and moose.
Northern Forests	Much of this area is wilderness with short, warm summers and long, cold winters. Tree types include conifers, poplar, birch, and aspen. Animals include raccoons, bobcats, lynx, deer, and bears. Tourism, forestry, mining, fishing, and dairy and vegetable farming are important here.
Northwestern Forested Mountains	Region includes coniferous forests and grasslands. Includes the headwaters of many major rivers and a number of mountain ranges. Animals include elks, moose, deer, and grizzly bears. Precipitation varies, depending upon the elevation. Cold and dry in the north but wet along the Pacific Coast. Lumbering operations, oil, mining, and tourism are important. Agriculture includes orchards and vineyards.
Marine West Coast Forests	Includes mountains, coastal plains, and many islands. Coastal areas have a large amount of precipitation that grows lush vegetation, including redwood forests. Higher elevations remain cool all year and have less vegetation. Economic activities include forestry and fishing. Climate is generally moderate due to the Pacific Ocean. Animals include elks, otters, and grizzly bears.
Eastern Temperate Forests	This region has a moderate climate, consistent precipitation throughout the year, and lush forests. Trees include oak, maple, beech, and ash mixed with conifers in some areas. Wildlife includes porcupines, foxes, bobcats, and black bears. The area is full of large, urban centers that include about 40 percent of the population of North America. Economic activities include farming, manufacturing, forestry, and mining.

Ecoregions of North America

Great Plains	This area is mostly grassland with generally few changes in elevation and few forests. It has a dry climate and may have severe droughts. The northern plains have important wetlands for migratory birds. This is an important area for farming and ranching as well as mining and oil operations.
North American Deserts	Landforms include plains, mountains, hills, and mesas. Region has very little rainfall and little vegetation. Plant types are mostly sagebrush and cacti. Temperature is very hot in the day and very cold at night. Animals include mule deer, pronghorn antelope, rattlesnakes, and lizards. Some areas have irrigated agriculture including apples, grapefruit, wheat, and cotton. Other economic activities include mining and tourism.
Mediterranean California	This area has mild, rainy winters and hot, dry summers, including frequent droughts. It receives more rain than the desert, so it has a wider variety of plants, which include scrub oak and chaparral. The area consists of mountains, hills, mesas, and plains. It is heavily populated. Economic activities include valuable vegetable and fruit crops and manufacturing. Wildlife includes coyotes, California condors, and green sea turtles.
Southern Semi-Arid Highlands	Generally dry climate with common landforms such as hills, valleys, and plains. Mostly grasslands with some forests. Wildlife includes quails, doves, hares, jackrabbits, foxes, coyotes, deer, and pronghorn antelope. Ranching is important to this region. Silver, gold, lead, copper, and iron are mined here.
Temperate Sierras	Landforms include mountains, canyons, and foothills. Trees include mostly conifers and oaks. Wildlife includes wolves, cougars, coyotes, squirrels, mice, hummingbirds, and woodpeckers. Common crops include corn, beans, barley, wheat and oats. Cattle and sheep are also raised here.
Tropical Dry Forests	Much rain, especially in the summer, and high temperature all year. Plants include deciduous forests. Wildlife includes hares, squirrels, lynx, and deer. Much of the land area of this region is devoted to agriculture. Important products include cattle, pigs, poultry, wheat, and corn.
Tropical Wet Forests	High precipitation and very warm climate. Has very diverse plant and animal life. Wildlife includes squirrels, lynx, frogs, and alligators or crocodiles. Common birds include pheasant, parrots, and toucans. Agricultural crops include corn, beans, bananas, sugar cane, coffee, rice, and cattle. Tourism is very important in some tropical regions.

State Names and Abbreviations

State Name	Abbreviation	State Name	Abbreviation
Alabama	AL	Montana	MT
Alaska	AK	Nebraska	NE
Arizona	AZ	Nevada	NV
Arkansas	AR	New Hampshire	NH
California	CA	New Jersey	NJ
Colorado	CO	New Mexico	NM
Connecticut	CT	New York	NY
Delaware	DE	North Carolina	NC
Florida	FL	North Dakota	ND
Georgia	GA	Ohio	OH
Hawaii	HI	Oklahoma	OK
Idaho	ID	Oregon	OR
Illinois	IL	Pennsylvania	PA
Indiana	IN	Rhode Island	RI
Iowa	IA	South Carolina	SC
Kansas	KS	South Dakota	SD
Kentucky	KY	Tennessee	TN
Louisiana	LA	Texas	TX
Maine	ME	Utah	UT
Maryland	MD	Vermont	VT
Massachusetts	MA	Virginia	VA
Michigan	MI	Washington	WA
Minnesota	MN	West Virginia	WV
Mississippi	MS	Wisconsin	WI
Missouri	MO	Wyoming	WY

Glossary

A

abolitionist: a person who believed in abolishing slavery in the United States and its territories in the 1800s

anthropologist: a scientist who studies human beings and their ancestors

aquatic ecoregion: an ecoregion that is in water

aquifer: underground areas where water collects

archaeologist: a scientist who studies fossils and other remains of human cultures

artillery: heavy guns used to bombard enemy positions from a distance with explosive shells

B

basin: an area of lower elevation that drains the surrounding land

biodiversity: the variety of plant and animal species living in a certain area

brownfields: abandoned industrial sites that are often polluted

C

cardinal directions: the four main directions (north, south, east, and west)

cave: a natural opening in the earth that is large enough for a human to enter

census: a count of the U.S. population that takes place every ten years

chronological order: events listed in order in which they happen

climate: the typical weather of a specific place on Earth

compass rose: a map symbol that shows directions

coniferous trees: trees, such as spruce and pine, that produce cones and needles rather than leaves

conquistador: Spanish soldiers and explorers who conquered much of North and South America for Spain between the 15th and 17th centuries

continent: a large land mass

D

data: information usually presented in numerical format

deciduous trees: trees, such as maple, that usually lose their leaves at some time in the year

E

economy: a system of making and transporting products and services

ecoregion: an area of land or water that has a collection of plants and animals that is unique to that area

electoral votes: votes cast by electors in a presidential election

electors: members of the Electoral College who cast votes for president

elevation: the height of the land, usually in relation to sea level

endangered: plants or animals that are threatened or in danger of dying out

equator: an imaginary line drawn around the center of Earth

erosion: the wearing away of land and soil by wind or the flow of water

expedition: a long, organized journey often through an unexplored area

extinct: a type of animal that no longer exists

fossil fuels: fuels, such as oil, coal, and natural gas, created in the ground from the ancient remains of plants and animals

frontier: the far edge of a country, where few people live

geography: the study of Earth in all its variety

glacier: huge, slow-moving masses of ice

globe: a representation of Earth in miniature that imitates its round shape

habitat: the places where plants and animals live

hemisphere: half of a globe

historical map: a map that shows past events or early political boundaries

hydropower: electrical energy from the flow of water captured by turbines at a hydroelectric plant

immigrant: a person who permanently relocates to a new country

inset map: a smaller map within a larger map that shows additional information

intermediate directions: directions that are between the cardinal directions (northeast, southeast, northwest, and southwest)

invasive species: plants or animals that have been introduced to an area where they do not occur naturally and have a negative effect on native species

karst: a landscape that includes sinkholes and disappearing streams and is usually evidence of caves

landform: the shape or form of a physical feature of Earth's surface (for example, a plain, hill, or mountain)

land-use plan: A plan to control development that helps communities preserve the environment

latitude: lines on a map or globe drawn east to west, parallel to the equator

longitude: lines on a map or globe drawn from north to south, parallel to the prime meridian

manifest destiny: the belief that it was inevitable that the United States would expand west to the Pacific Ocean

map: a flat representation of Earth

map legend: a box on a map that explains what each symbol on the map means

map title: a label that identifies the subject of a map

military campaign: the movement of armed forces in planned offensive actions against an enemy during time of war

naturalist: a person who studies nature in the outdoors

North Pole: the most northern point on Earth

nuclear energy: energy generated from uranium

ocean: the large body of salt water that covers most of the surface of the earth

oral history: personal experiences usually collected through oral interviews

organism: a living thing; usually a plant or animal

petroglyphs: cave drawings by ancient human beings

physical map: a map that shows a region's landforms and water forms

political map: a map showing human political divisions of Earth's surface

precipitation: liquid or solid water that falls from the atmosphere to Earth

prime meridian: an imaginary line around Earth from top to bottom that runs through the city of Greenwich, England

reapportionment: the process of adjusting congressional representation every ten years based on population changes

satellite: a device made by human beings that orbits Earth for the purpose of collecting and communicating information

scale: the relationship of distance on a map to real-world distance showing how much smaller the map is than the real world

secede: to break away from or leave

siege: a military blockade of a city intended to prevent anyone from getting in or out

solar power: power from the heat of the sun captured by solar panels and converted to electricity

South Pole: the most southern point on Earth

speleology: the exploration and study of caves

suffrage movement: a political movement in the late 1800s and early 1900s to get state and federal governments to grant voting rights to women

symbols: drawings, lines, or dots on a map that stand for something else

temperance movement: a political movement in the early 1900s against the manufacture and use of alcohol resulting in the Eighteenth Amendment to the U.S. Constitution

temperate ecoregions: mid-latitude ecoregions that usually do not experience the temperature extremes of northern or southern latitudes

terrestrial ecoregion: an ecoregion that is on land

thematic map: a map that explains important things about people

time line: a list of important events, usually in chronological order

tributary: a smaller stream that joins a larger stream

troglobites: animals that live only in caves and cannot survive anywhere else

troglophiles: animals that mostly dwell in caves but have the capability of living in other locations

trogloxenes: animals that occasionally use caves for shelter

tropical ecoregions: warm and humid ecoregions that lie close to the equator

tundra: a treeless plain that supports mostly grasses, mosses, and shrubs

turbine: a rotor with blades and a shaft, like a fan, that captures the energy from wind, water, or other some source, so it can be converted to electricity

urban sprawl: the uncontrolled or unplanned growth of urban areas into the countryside

water form: the shape, form, or nature of a specific physical feature of water on Earth (for example, a river, lake, or ocean)

watershed: area of land that separates water flowing into different bodies of water

wind power: power from wind captured by turbines and turned into electrical energy

wetlands: land that is usually wet or flooded much of the year

Index

Answer Key

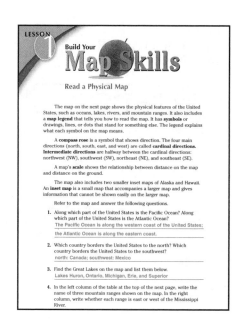

Page 4 — LESSON 1: Build Your Map Skills — Read a Physical Map

The map on the next page shows the physical features of the United States, such as oceans, lakes, rivers, and mountain ranges. It also includes a **map legend** that tells you how to read the map. It has **symbols** or drawings, lines, or dots that stand for something else. The legend explains what each symbol on the map means.

A **compass rose** is a symbol that shows direction. The four main directions (north, south, east, and west) are called **cardinal directions.** **Intermediate directions** are halfway between the cardinal directions: northwest (NW), southwest (SW), northeast (NE), and southeast (SE).

A map's **scale** shows the relationship between distance on the map and distance on the ground.

The map also includes two smaller inset maps of Alaska and Hawaii. An **inset map** is a small map that accompanies a larger map and gives information that cannot be shown easily on the larger map.

Refer to the map and answer the following questions.

1. Along which part of the United States is the Pacific Ocean? Along which part of the United States is the Atlantic Ocean?
   The Pacific Ocean is along the western coast of the United States;
   the Atlantic Ocean is along the eastern coast.

2. Which country borders the United States to the north? Which country borders the United States to the southwest?
   north: Canada; southwest: Mexico

3. Find the Great Lakes on the map and list them below.
   Lakes Huron, Ontario, Michigan, Erie, and Superior

4. In the left column of the table at the top of the next page, write the name of three mountain ranges shown on the map. In the right column, write whether each range is east or west of the Mississippi River.

4

Page 5

Mountain Range	East or West?
Appalachian Mountains	east
Rocky Mountains	west
Cascade Mountains	west

5. Use the map to complete the table below.

River	The river flows in which direction?	The river flows into which body of water?
Missouri	east then southeast	Mississippi River
Columbia	west	Pacific Ocean
Ohio	southwest	Mississippi River
Arkansas	southeast	Mississippi River
Brazos	southeast then south	Gulf of Mexico
Colorado	southwest	Gulf of California
Platte	southeast then northeast	Missouri River

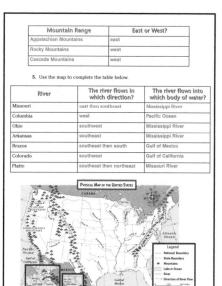

PHYSICAL MAP OF THE UNITED STATES

5

Page 6 — LESSON 1: Explore North America

Something to Think About: How do you think people traveled long ago without maps to guide them?

When the first people arrived in North America from Europe, the continent had not been divided into countries. In the area that later became the United States, there were no state boundaries. These people navigated from place to place mostly based on landmarks, or the physical features of the land.

Early European explorers of North America hiked across the land or floated on boats or rafts. Rivers were a good way to travel. Rivers could carry people downstream, sometimes for hundreds of miles. As you learned from the map on page 5, all rivers flow into another body of water such as a lake, an ocean, or another river.

In this activity, you will navigate across the United States from coast to coast just like these early people, though they did not have a modern map. You will begin your journey at the star on the northeast coast. You will end your journey at the star on the northwest coast.

1. Plan your trip by drawing lines on the map on the next page with a colored pencil. The lines you will draw will show the way you will travel. From the star on the northeast coast, draw a line southwest to the Appalachian Mountains in Ohio.

   The starting point (at the star) is between which two rivers?
   The star is between the Hudson and Connecticut rivers.

   Which ocean lies to the east?
   The Atlantic Ocean lies to the east.

   What major water features lie to the north?
   the Great Lakes

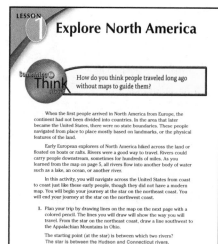

6

Page 7

2. You decide to raft down the Ohio River. In which general direction will you travel? Into which river does the Ohio River flow?
   I will be traveling southwest. The Ohio River flows into the
   Mississippi River.

3. From the place where the Ohio River ends, you decide to head northwest. Which two major rivers will you encounter as you cross the plains before you reach the Rocky Mountains?
   the Missouri and Platte rivers

4. When you reach Idaho, follow the Snake River until it turns north. At this point, leave the river and continue traveling northwest.

   Which mountain range will you encounter in Washington and Oregon?
   the Cascades

   What river will you encounter before you reach your final destination?
   the Columbia River

   Into which body of water does this river empty?
   the Pacific Ocean

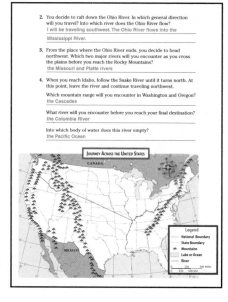

JOURNEY ACROSS THE UNITED STATES

7

Page 11

The results of the full census are very important because the population of the country influences the way it is governed. For example, the number of representatives each state is allowed to send to the House of Representatives is determined by the state's population.

Refer to Map 1 on page 9 and to Map 2 on page 10 to answer the following questions.

1. Which two states have more than 20 million people? Use the compass rose to tell where they are located within the U.S.
   California and Texas have more than 20 million people. California
   is located on the west coast of the continental United States; it is
   just south of Oregon. Texas is located in the south-central
   United States; it is south of Oklahoma and New Mexico.

2. Which two states experienced the fastest rate of population growth from 1990 to 2000? Use the compass rose to tell where they are located within the United States.
   Arizona and Nevada experienced the fastest rate of population
   growth over this period; both states are located in the
   southwestern United States.

3. What was the rate of population growth in the United States as a whole between 1990 and 2000? How do you know? Did most states exceed this rate?
   According to the Map 1 legend, the population grew 13.2 percent
   during this period. Most states did not exceed this rate.

4. Examine Map 1 carefully. What conclusions can you draw about population growth in the United States based on the map?
   Possible response: Population growth in northern and midwestern
   states is slow; growth in southern and southwestern states is high.

5. A classmate looks at Map 1 and tells you that Pennsylvania is one of the least populous U.S. states. Is your classmate correct? Explain why or why not.
   The classmate is incorrect. Map 1 does not illustrate population—
   it illustrates population growth. The population of Pennsylvania
   is not increasing at a rapid rate, but as Map 2 shows, the state is
   actually one of the most populous in the country.

11

Page 12 — LESSON 2: Understand Data in Charts

Something to Think About: How can data help you to learn about the people of the United States?

The U.S. Census Bureau has a big job! Besides counting the population, the U.S. Census Bureau collects many other types of information about people. This includes information about births, deaths, jobs, family income, housing, education, and the movement of people from place to place. This type of information, called **data**, is constantly changing.

The data from the U.S. Census Bureau are intended to give you a mental picture of the people of the United States. For example, over time, the number of people in certain age groups changes. Chart 1 shows the changes that took place between the years 1990 and 2000. Each age group in Chart 1 is shown as a percentage of the total U.S. population. Chart 2 shows the percentage of Americans age 25 and older who have graduated from high school or college. People under the age of 25 are not included in the data shown in Chart 2.

Refer to both charts to answer the following questions.

1. How many age groups are shown in Chart 1?
   10

2. What is the youngest age group in Chart 1? The oldest?
   The youngest is Under 5; the oldest is 85+.

3. In Chart 1, what do the brown bars show in each age category? What do the green bars show?
   The brown bars show the percentage of Americans who were a
   particular age in 1990; the green bars show the percentage in 2000.

12

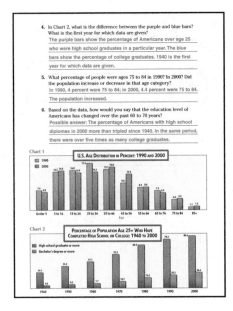

4. In Chart 2, what is the difference between the purple and blue bars? What is the first year for which data are given?
The purple bars show the percentage of Americans over age 25 who were high school graduates in a particular year. The blue bars show the percentage of college graduates. 1940 is the first year for which data are given.

5. What percentage of people were ages 75 to 84 in 1990? In 2000? Did the population increase or decrease in that age category?
In 1990, 4 percent were 75 to 84; in 2000, 4.4 percent were 75 to 84. The population increased.

6. Based on the data, how would you say that the education level of Americans has changed over the past 60 to 70 years?
Possible answer: The percentage of Americans with high school diplomas in 2000 more than tripled since 1940. In the same period, there were over five times as many college graduates.

13

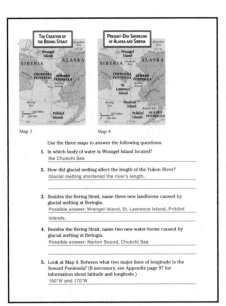

Use the three maps to answer the following questions.

1. In which body of water is Wrangel Island located?
the Chukchi Sea

2. How did glacial melting affect the length of the Yukon River?
Glacial melting shortened the river's length.

3. Besides the Bering Strait, name three new landforms caused by glacial melting at Beringia.
Possible answer: Wrangel Island, St. Lawrence Island, Pribilof Islands

4. Besides the Bering Strait, name two new water forms caused by glacial melting at Beringia.
Possible answer: Norton Sound, Chukchi Sea

5. Look at Map 4. Between what two major lines of longitude is the Seward Peninsula? (If necessary, see Appendix page 97 for information about latitude and longitude.)
160°W and 170°W

17

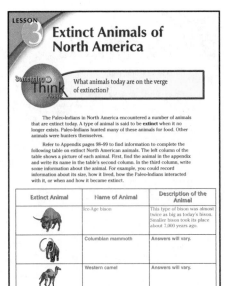

LESSON 3 — Extinct Animals of North America

Something to Think About: What animals today are on the verge of extinction?

The Paleo-Indians in North America encountered a number of animals that are extinct today. A type of animal is said to be **extinct** when it no longer exists. Paleo-Indians hunted many of these animals for food. Other animals were hunters themselves.

Refer to Appendix pages 98–99 to find information to complete the following table on extinct North American animals. The left column of the table shows a picture of each animal. First, find the animal in the appendix and write its name in the table's second column. In the third column, write some information about the animal. For example, you could record information about its size, how it lived, how the Paleo-Indians interacted with it, or when and how it became extinct.

Extinct Animal	Name of Animal	Description of the Animal
	Ice-Age bison	This type of bison was almost twice as big as today's bison. Smaller bison took its place about 7,000 years ago.
	Columbian mammoth	Answers will vary.
	Western camel	Answers will vary.

18

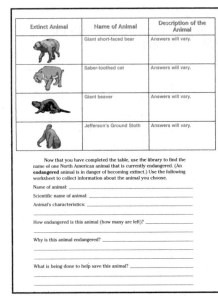

Extinct Animal	Name of Animal	Description of the Animal
	Giant short-faced bear	Answers will vary.
	Saber-toothed cat	Answers will vary.
	Giant beaver	Answers will vary.
	Jefferson's Ground Sloth	Answers will vary.

Now that you have completed the table, use the library to find the name of one North American animal that is currently endangered. (An **endangered** animal is in danger of becoming extinct.) Use the following worksheet to collect information about the animal you choose.

Name of animal: _____
Scientific name of animal: _____
Animal's characteristics: _____
How endangered is this animal (how many are left)? _____
Why is this animal endangered? _____
What is being done to help save this animal? _____

19

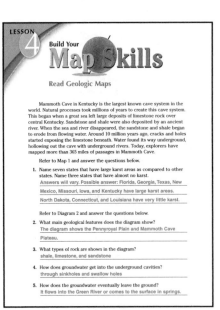

LESSON 4 — Build Your Map Skills

Read Geologic Maps

Mammoth Cave in Kentucky is the largest known cave system in the world. Natural processes took millions of years to create this cave system. This began when a great sea left large deposits of limestone rock over central Kentucky. Sandstone and shale were also deposited by an ancient river. When the sea and river disappeared, the sandstone and shale began to erode from flowing water. Around 10 million years ago, cracks and holes started exposing the limestone beneath. Water found its way underground, hollowing out the cave with underground rivers. Today, explorers have mapped more than 365 miles of passages in Mammoth Cave.

Refer to Map 1 and answer the questions below.

1. Name seven states that have large karst areas as compared to other states. Name three states that have almost no karst.
Answers will vary. Possible answer: Florida, Georgia, Texas, New Mexico, Missouri, Iowa, and Kentucky have large karst areas. North Dakota, Connecticut, and Louisiana have very little karst.

Refer to Diagram 2 and answer the questions below.

2. What main geological features does the diagram show?
The diagram shows the Pennyroyal Plain and Mammoth Cave Plateau.

3. What types of rock are shown in the diagram?
shale, limestone, and sandstone

4. How does groundwater get into the underground cavities?
through sinkholes and swallow holes

5. How does the groundwater eventually leave the ground?
It flows into the Green River or comes to the surface in springs.

22

LESSON 4 — Cave Dwelling Animals

Something to Think About: Why is it important to protect cave environments?

Caves provide shelter and habitat for many animals. There are three categories of cave-dwelling animals. **Trogloxenes** sometimes use caves for shelter but often dwell outside the cave environment. **Troglophiles** live most of their lives in caves but have the capability of living in other locations. **Troglobites** live only in caves and can't survive anywhere else. Over 200 species of animals live in Mammoth Cave alone.

The environment in caves is special. It doesn't change as rapidly as the outside world. The lack of light inside a cave limits plant growth and the availability of food.

Animals that live only in caves have adapted to their environment. The populations of cave animals tend to be small, and they usually have slow rates of growth and reproduction. The lack of light also has caused many cave animals to lack both pigment (they have no coloration) and sight.

Use the information above to answer the following questions about cave animals.

1. Why do you think the population of cave animals is usually small?
Because there is not much food inside a cave.

2. What advantage could a troglobite have over its cousins that live on the surface of Earth?
Possible answer: greater safety from predators

3. Look at the picture of each animal in the table. See if you can determine by looking at the animal if it is a trogloxene, a troglophile, or a troglobite. Write your answers in the table.

24

Page 25

Animal	Animal Name	Trogl[o]xene, Troglophile, or Troglobite?
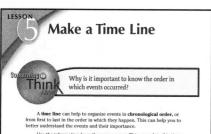 Raccoon	Raccoon	Trogloxene
	Blind crayfish	Troglobite
	Camel backed cave cricket	Troglophile
	Blind Texas salamander	Troglobite
	Little brown bat	Trogloxene
	Blind millipede	Troglobite
	Blind flatworm	Troglobite
	Blind cave beetle	Troglophile
	Adult cave salamander	Troglophile

25

Page 28

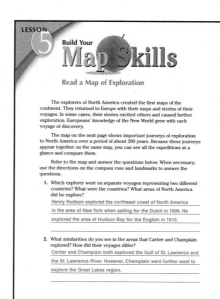

LESSON 5 — Build Your Map Skills

Read a Map of Exploration

The explorers of North America created the first maps of the continent. They returned to Europe with their maps and stories of their voyages. In some cases, their stories excited others and caused further exploration. Europeans' knowledge of the New World grew with each voyage of discovery.

The map on the next page shows important journeys of exploration to North America over a period of about 200 years. Because these journeys appear together on the same map, you can see all the expeditions at a glance and compare them.

Refer to the map and answer the questions below. When necessary, use the directions on the compass rose and landmarks to answer the questions.

1. Which explorer went on separate voyages representing two different countries? What were the countries? What areas of North America did he explore?
   Henry Hudson explored the northeast coast of North America in the area of New York when sailing for the Dutch in 1609. He explored the area of Hudson Bay for the English in 1610.

2. What similarities do you see in the areas that Cartier and Champlain explored? How did their voyages differ?
   Cartier and Champlain both explored the Gulf of St. Lawrence and the St. Lawrence River. However, Champlain went further west to explore the Great Lakes region.

28

Page 29

3. What area did Coronado explore in 1540–1542? Describe his journey as it appears on the map.
   The Coronado expedition traveled north along the western coast of Mexico, and it turned northeast to enter what is now Arizona. Members of the expedition discovered the Colorado River and the Grand Canyon. The expedition then headed east across New Mexico, Texas, Oklahoma, and Kansas.

4. Describe the important expedition that took place in 1524.
   Verrazzano explored the east coast of North America. He sailed from the Carolinas all the way to Newfoundland.

5. Who was the first European to see the Mississippi River? How can you tell this from the map?
   De Soto was the first European to see the Mississippi River. He explored the southeastern United States in 1539–1541. This was before the two other Mississippi River expeditions on the map.

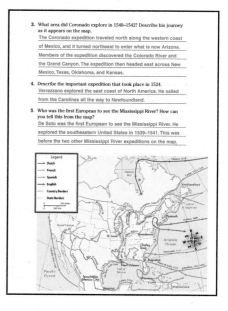

29

Page 30

LESSON 5 — Make a Time Line

Something to Think About
Why is it important to know the order in which events occurred?

A **time line** can help to organize events in **chronological order**, or from first to last in the order in which they happen. This can help you to better understand the events and their importance.

Use the information from the map on page 29 to complete this time line. Write each explorer's name in the time line. When an expedition covers a range of years (for example, 1540–1542), put items in chronological order based on the first year in the range. The first two items have been completed for you.

Years	Explorer	Country
1492–1493	Columbus	Spanish
1513	Ponce de León	Spanish
1519	Cortés	Spanish
1524	Verrazzano	Spanish
1535–1536	Cartier	French
1539–1541	De Soto	Spanish
1540–1542	Coronado	Spanish
1542–1543	Cabrillo	Spanish
1603–1613	Champlain	French
1609	Hudson	Dutch
1610	Hudson	English
1673	Joliet and Marquette	French
1679–1682	La Salle	French

30

Page 31

Answer the following questions. If necessary, refer again to the previous pages of this lesson.

1. What were some of the dangers of a voyage of exploration to the New World?
   The voyage across the Atlantic was long and difficult. Ships were frequently destroyed or became lost. Most of the explorers feared starvation and disease.

2. What was the purpose of the Joliet and Marquette expedition?
   Joliet and Marquette tried to find a passage down the Mississippi to the Gulf of California. Marquette wanted to teach Christianity to the Native Americans, and both explorers wanted to establish a fur trade.

3. What did the expeditions of Coronado and Cortés have in common? Were they successful? Explain.
   Both Coronado and Cortés wished to take riches from the Native Americans. Cortés was successful. He conquered the Aztec empire and acquired great riches. Coronado was unsuccessful. He sought Cibola, the cities of gold, which did not exist.

4. Select an expedition you have read about in this lesson. Do some library research to find more details about it. Answer the following questions about the expedition on a separate sheet of paper.
   • What was the explorer's name? Who sponsored or encouraged the expedition? When did it take place?
   • How many people went on the journey? How did they travel?
   • What was the goal or purpose of the expedition? Did the goal change during the explorer's travels? If so, how did it change?
   • The explorers traveled through what areas of North America?
   • What difficulties did the expedition encounter?
   • Why was the expedition important enough for later generations to remember?

31

Page 34

LESSON 6 — Build Your Map Skills

Conflict in the Colonies

After their victory in the French and Indian War, many colonists believed they had strong claims to most of the land up to the Mississippi River. These colonists were eager to move west and establish towns and trading posts.

As you have already learned, the Native Americans who lived along the frontier did not welcome the British, including the colonists. The British government wanted to make peace along the frontier to make it easier and less costly to defend it. To calm Native American worries that colonists would force them from their lands, the British issued the Proclamation of 1763. The Proclamation restricted colonial settlement west of the Appalachian Mountains.

Most colonists deeply resented the Proclamation. They thought they were entitled to move into these western lands. Colonists saw the Proclamation as another example of the British government's meddling in their affairs—a feeling of resentment that would build until it exploded into the Revolutionary War.

Refer to Map 2 and answer the following questions.

1. Describe the areas shown on the map where German immigrants settled.
   Germans settled in Pennsylvania, west of Philadelphia; in northern Virginia; and in upper New York.

2. Describe the ethnic makeup of the Southern Colonies.
   The Southern Colonies consisted largely of English, Scotch-Irish, and Africans, with smaller pockets of German settlers.

3. Which ethnic group settled along the Hudson River?
   the Dutch

34

Answer Key

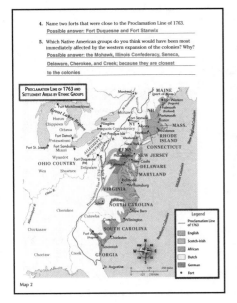

(Page 35 content)

4. Name two forts that were close to the Proclamation Line of 1763.
   Possible answer: Fort Duquesne and Fort Stanwix

5. Which Native American groups do you think would have been most immediately affected by the western expansion of the colonies? Why?
   Possible answer: the Mohawk, Illinois Confederacy, Seneca, Delaware, Cherokee, and Creek; because they are closest to the colonies

PROCLAMATION LINE OF 1763 AND SETTLEMENT AREAS BY ETHNIC GROUPS

Map 2

(Page 37 content)

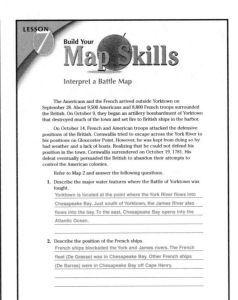

Colony	Founded by	New England, Middle, or Southern?	Important Facts
Connecticut Year Founded: 1635	Thomas Hooker	New England	This colony created the Fundamental Orders of Connecticut in 1639, partly the basis for the U.S. Constitution.
Delaware Year Founded: 1638	the New Sweden Company and Peter Minuit	Middle	Answers will vary.
Georgia Year Founded: 1732	James Edward Oglethorpe	Southern	
Maryland Year Founded: 1634	Lord Baltimore	Southern	
Massachusetts Year Founded: 1620	the Puritans	New England	
New Hampshire Year Founded: 1623	John Wheelwright	New England	
New Jersey Year Founded: 1664	Lord Berkeley and Sir George Carteret	Middle	
New York Year Founded: 1664	Duke of York	Middle	
North Carolina Year Founded: 1653	Virginians	Southern	
Pennsylvania Year Founded: 1682	William Penn	Middle	
Rhode Island Year Founded: 1636	Roger Williams	New England	
South Carolina Year Founded: 1663	Nobles with a royal charter from Charles II	Southern	
Virginia Year Founded: 1607	London Company	Southern	

(Page 40 content)

LESSON 7
Build Your Map Skills

Interpret a Battle Map

The Americans and the French arrived outside Yorktown on September 28. About 9,500 Americans and 8,800 French troops surrounded the British. On October 9, they began an artillery bombardment of Yorktown that destroyed much of the town and set fire to British ships in the harbor.

On October 14, French and American troops attacked the defensive positions of the British. Cornwallis tried to escape across the York River to his positions on Gloucester Point. However, he was kept from doing so by bad weather and a lack of boats. Realizing that he could not defend his position in the town, Cornwallis surrendered on October 19, 1781. His defeat eventually persuaded the British to abandon their attempts to control the American colonies.

Refer to Map 2 and answer the following questions.

1. Describe the major water features where the Battle of Yorktown was fought.
   Yorktown is located at the point where the York River flows into Chesapeake Bay. Just south of Yorktown, the James River also flows into the bay. To the east, Chesapeake Bay opens into the Atlantic Ocean.

2. Describe the position of the French ships.
   French ships blockaded the York and James rivers. The French fleet (De Grasse) was in Chesapeake Bay. Other French ships (De Barras) were in Chesapeake Bay off Cape Henry.

40

(Page 41 content)

3. Where were the French and American troops positioned around Yorktown during the siege?
   The French were on the northwest side of Yorktown in a semicircle extending around the town from the York River. The Americans were on the southeast side of the town extending from Wormley Creek toward the French.

4. Besides their positions at Yorktown, what other area did British, American, and French troops occupy?
   British, American, and French troops were also at Gloucester Point across the York River from Yorktown.

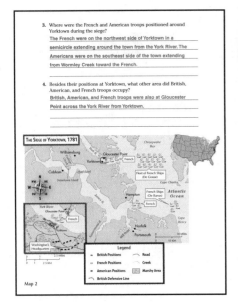

THE SIEGE OF YORKTOWN, 1781

Map 2

41

(Page 42 content)

LESSON 7
Organize Information

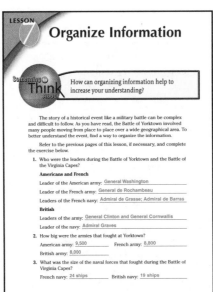

Something to Think About

How can organizing information help to increase your understanding?

The story of a historical event like a military battle can be complex and difficult to follow. As you have read, the Battle of Yorktown involved many people moving from place to place over a wide geographical area. To better understand the event, find a way to organize the information.

Refer to the previous pages of this lesson, if necessary, and complete the exercise below.

1. Who were the leaders during the Battle of Yorktown and the Battle of the Virginia Capes?

   Americans and French

   Leader of the American army: General Washington

   Leader of the French army: General de Rochambeau

   Leaders of the French navy: Admiral de Grasse; Admiral de Barras

   British

   Leaders of the army: General Clinton and General Cornwallis

   Leader of the navy: Admiral Graves

2. How big were the armies that fought at Yorktown?

   American army: 9,500   French army: 8,800

   British army: 8,000

3. What was the size of the naval forces that fought during the Battle of Virginia Capes?

   French navy: 24 ships   British navy: 19 ships

42

(Page 43 content)

4. When and where were the battles fought?
   Battle of Virginia Capes: September 5–9, 1781
   Where: Off Chesapeake Bay along the Virginia coast
   Siege and Battle of Yorktown: September 28 to October 19
   Where: Yorktown and Gloucester, Virginia

5. Why did General Cornwallis move his troops to Yorktown?
   He wanted to establish a naval base there. At Yorktown, he could receive supplies and even be evacuated by ship.

6. Why did General Washington and General Rochambeau move their armies south to Virginia from New York?
   They received news that Admiral de Grasse was coming to Chesapeake Bay with a large fleet, including troops. Since the British forces under Cornwallis were in Virginia, this presented a good opportunity to fight them.

7. What was the result of the Battle of Virginia Capes? Why was this battle important?
   British and French naval forces fought off Chesapeake Bay. The French fleet was able to drive off the British fleet. This was important because it isolated the forces of Cornwallis at Yorktown. He could not receive supplies or reinforcements from the sea or be evacuated.

8. What was important about the arrival of the ships of Admiral de Barras at Chesapeake Bay?
   The ships of De Barras brought additional French troops to help in the coming battle. De Barras also brought artillery that the French and Americans used to bombard the British positions.

9. Overall, why was the Battle of Yorktown important to the American War of Independence?
   The surrender of the British forces at Yorktown persuaded the British to abandon their struggle to control the American colonies.

Answer Key

Page 46

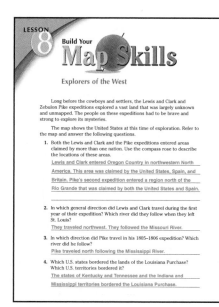

LESSON 8

Build Your Map Skills

Explorers of the West

Long before the cowboys and settlers, the Lewis and Clark and Zebulon Pike expeditions explored a vast land that was largely unknown and unmapped. The people on these expeditions had to be brave and strong to explore its mysteries.

The map shows the United States at this time of exploration. Refer to the map and answer the following questions.

1. Both the Lewis and Clark and the Pike expeditions entered areas claimed by more than one nation. Use the compass rose to describe the locations of these areas.
   Lewis and Clark entered Oregon Country in northwestern North America. This area was claimed by the United States, Spain, and Britain. Pike's second expedition entered a region north of the Rio Grande that was claimed by both the United States and Spain.

2. In which general direction did Lewis and Clark travel during the first year of their expedition? Which river did they follow when they left St. Louis?
   They traveled northwest. They followed the Missouri River.

3. In which direction did Pike travel in his 1805–1806 expedition? Which river did he follow?
   Pike traveled north following the Mississippi River.

4. Which U.S. states bordered the lands of the Louisiana Purchase? Which U.S. territories bordered it?
   The states of Kentucky and Tennessee and the Indiana and Mississippi territories bordered the Louisiana Purchase.

Page 47

5. During their return trip in 1806, Lewis and Clark became separated for a time. Which one of them took the more northerly route?
   Lewis took the more northerly route.

6. Use the compass rose and landmarks to describe the route of Pike's second expedition.
   Pike left St. Louis traveling west and then northwest. He turned southwest and followed the Arkansas River west to Pike's Peak. He continued north to the South Platte River and then headed south into Spanish Territory along the Rio Grande. He traveled south to Chihuahua, northeast to San Antonio, and finally to Natchitoches at the edge of Louisiana Territory.

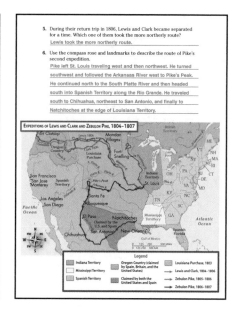

Expeditions of Lewis and Clark and Zebulon Pike, 1804–1807

Legend
- Indiana Territory
- Mississippi Territory
- Spanish Territory
- Oregon Country (claimed by Spain, Britain, and the United States)
- Claimed by both the United States and Spain
- Louisiana Purchase, 1803
- Lewis and Clark, 1804–1806
- Zebulon Pike, 1805–1806
- Zebulon Pike, 1806–1807

Page 48

LESSON 8

Defend the Louisiana Purchase

Something to Think About Why is it important to debate the actions of the government?

Refer to the previous pages of this lesson, if necessary, and answer the questions below.

1. Why did France decide to sell the Louisiana Territory to the United States?
   France anticipated a war with Britain and was short of cash.

2. What were two major reasons why President Jefferson decided to send Lewis and Clark on an expedition to the Northwest?
   Possible answer: He wanted to strengthen U.S. claims to Oregon Country by sending an expedition there. He also wanted to explore the possibilities for commerce.

3. Before the Louisiana Purchase was made, why was the French-owned city of New Orleans important to the United States?
   New Orleans was a key port on the Mississippi River. The United States wanted to purchase it to help keep the Mississippi River open for commerce.

You will become an expert on the Louisiana Purchase and its exploration. To start, reread the material in this lesson and on Appendix page 101 about the Lewis and Clark expedition. Then, go to the library for further research. Read through at least one more source describing facts about the Louisiana Purchase and the Corps of Discovery.

Page 49

Now, after your reading and research, you are ready to assume the role of someone just returning from the expedition with the Corps of Discovery. Some members of Congress are asking President Jefferson why the Louisiana Purchase was a good idea. They are wondering why Jefferson bought these lands that are so far away from settled areas. They ask, "How will the Louisiana Territory, a remote wilderness, benefit the United States?" They have also asked President Jefferson to explain the purpose of the Corps of Discovery expedition.

As a special assistant to President Jefferson, you must help write a persuasive argument. In the space below, explain why the Louisiana Purchase was a good idea. Describe why the new western lands are an asset to the nation. Describe the successful results of the Corps of Discovery expedition. Try to convince the skeptical members of Congress that the United States is better off with these new lands.

Answers will vary. Possible answer: The Mississippi River and the port of New Orleans are essential for trade, especially for the western states and territories. The purchase of the Louisiana Territory helps to ensure that the Mississippi River will be open to U.S. commerce in the future.

The addition of the Louisiana Territory more than doubles the size of the United States. It will ensure that our nation has room to expand. Future generations will look at this investment as one of the smartest purchases in history.

The Corps of Discovery has engaged in an essential expedition to map this new land and to understand the native people and natural resources there. Our expedition made contacts with native people, which will be the basis for future trade. In our journals, we collected important information about many animals, plants, and other natural resources that may one day help feed our country.

We journeyed through Oregon Country to the Pacific Ocean. Our travels in this region helped to strengthen U.S. claims to these important lands that one day might give us a connection to the west coast and the vast ocean there with its possibilities for seaports and trade.

Page 52

LESSON 9

Build Your Map Skills

Our Nation in Crisis

The maps tell the story of the debate and compromise that eventually led to the war between the North and South. Reread pages 50–51, if necessary. Refer to the maps, and answer the following questions.

1. At the time of the Compromise of 1850, how many slave states were there? How many free states?
   There were 15 slave states and 15 free states.

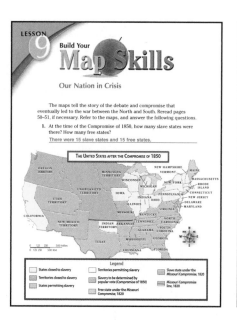

The United States after the Compromise of 1850

Legend
- States closed to slavery
- Territories closed to slavery
- States permitting slavery
- Territories permitting slavery
- Slavery to be determined by popular vote (Compromise of 1850)
- Free state under the Missouri Compromise, 1820
- Slave state under the Missouri Compromise, 1820
- Missouri Compromise line, 1820

Page 53

2. Name the slave states that were situated north of the Missouri Compromise line.
   Missouri, Kentucky, Virginia, Maryland, and Delaware

3. What changes took place in the Unorganized Territory between 1850 and 1854?
   In 1850, the Unorganized Territory was closed to slavery. By 1854, the area had been divided into the Nebraska Territory and Kansas Territory, and slavery was to be determined by popular vote.

4. After the Kansas-Nebraska Act, which free states shared a border with at least one slave state?
   Iowa, Illinois, Indiana, Ohio, Pennsylvania, New Jersey

5. Was the Kansas-Nebraska Act a victory for southern slaveholders or northern abolitionists? How do you know?
   It was a victory for southern slaveholders. It opened up previously free territory to the possibility of slavery.

The United States after the Kansas-Nebraska Act of 1854

Legend
- States closed to slavery
- Territories closed to slavery
- States permitting slavery
- Territories permitting slavery
- Slavery to be determined by popular vote (Compromise of 1850)
- Slavery to be determined by popular vote (Kansas-Nebraska Act 1854)

Answer Key

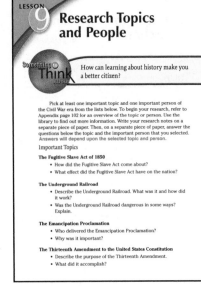

LESSON 9 — Research Topics and People

Something to Think About: How can learning about history make you a better citizen?

Pick at least one important topic and one important person of the Civil War era from the lists below. To begin your research, refer to Appendix page 102 for an overview of the topic or person. Use the library to find out more information. Write your research notes on a separate piece of paper. Then, on a separate piece of paper, answer the questions below the topic and the important person that you selected. Answers will depend upon the selected topic and person.

Important Topics

The Fugitive Slave Act of 1850
- How did the Fugitive Slave Act come about?
- What effect did the Fugitive Slave Act have on the nation?

The Underground Railroad
- Describe the Underground Railroad. What was it and how did it work?
- Was the Underground Railroad dangerous in some ways? Explain.

The Emancipation Proclamation
- Who delivered the Emancipation Proclamation?
- Why was it important?

The Thirteenth Amendment to the United States Constitution
- Describe the purpose of the Thirteenth Amendment.
- What did it accomplish?

54

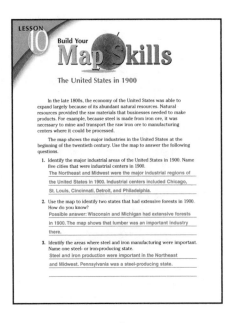

LESSON 10 — Build Your Map Skills

The United States in 1900

In the late 1800s, the economy of the United States was able to expand largely because of its abundant natural resources. Natural resources provided the raw materials that businesses needed to make products. For example, because steel is made from iron ore, it was necessary to mine and transport the raw iron ore to manufacturing centers where it could be processed.

The map shows the major industries in the United States at the beginning of the twentieth century. Use the map to answer the following questions.

1. Identify the major industrial areas of the United States in 1900. Name five cities that were industrial centers in 1900.
   The Northeast and Midwest were the major industrial regions of the United States in 1900. Industrial centers included Chicago, St. Louis, Cincinnati, Detroit, and Philadelphia.

2. Use the map to identify two states that had extensive forests in 1900. How do you know?
   Possible answer: Wisconsin and Michigan had extensive forests in 1900. The map shows that lumber was an important industry there.

3. Identify the areas where steel and iron manufacturing were important. Name one steel- or iron-producing state.
   Steel and iron production were important in the Northeast and Midwest. Pennsylvania was a steel-producing state.

58

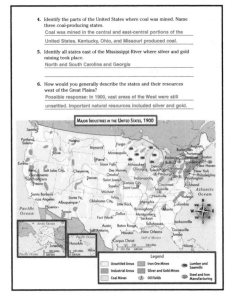

4. Identify the parts of the United States where coal was mined. Name three coal-producing states.
   Coal was mined in the central and east-central portions of the United States. Kentucky, Ohio, and Missouri produced coal.

5. Identify all states east of the Mississippi River where silver and gold mining took place.
   North and South Carolina and Georgia

6. How would you generally describe the states and their resources west of the Great Plains?
   Possible response: In 1900, vast areas of the West were still unsettled. Important natural resources included silver and gold.

Major Industries in the United States, 1900

Legend: Unsettled Areas, Industrial Areas, Coal Mines, Iron Ore Mines, Silver and Gold Mines, Oil Fields, Lumber and Sawmills, Steel and Iron Manufacturing

59

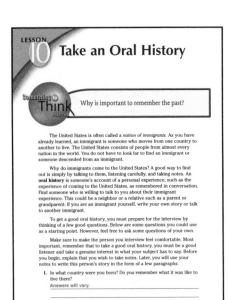

LESSON 10 — Take an Oral History

Something to Think About: Why is important to remember the past?

The United States is often called a *nation of immigrants*. As you have already learned, an immigrant is someone who moves from one country to another to live. The United States consists of people from almost every nation in the world. You do not have to look far to find an immigrant or someone descended from an immigrant.

Why do immigrants come to the United States? A good way to find out is simply by talking to them, listening carefully, and taking notes. An **oral history** is someone's account of a personal experience, such as the experience of coming to the United States, as remembered in conversation. Find someone who is willing to talk to you about their immigrant experience. This could be a neighbor or a relative such as a parent or grandparent. If you are an immigrant yourself, write your own story or talk to another immigrant.

To get a good oral history, you must prepare for the interview by thinking of a few good questions. Below are some questions you could use as a starting point. However, feel free to ask some questions of your own.

Make sure to make the person you interview feel comfortable. Most important, remember that to take a good oral history, you must be a good listener and take a genuine interest in what your subject has to say. Before you begin, explain that you wish to take notes. Later, you will use your notes to write this person's story in the form of a few paragraphs.

1. In what country were you born? Do you remember what it was like to live there?
   Answers will vary.

60

2. What occupation did you have in your native country? Did you work at a job or go to school?
   Answers will vary.

3. When did you come to the United States?
   Answers will vary.

4. In what state and city do you live now? Why did you choose that place to live of all the communities in the United States?
   Answers will vary.

5. Why did you decide to leave your native country?
   Answers will vary.

6. What do you miss about your native country? Do you still have relatives there?
   Answers will vary.

7. What things have worked out best for you since you arrived in the United States? What things could be better?
   Answers will vary.

8. Read through the answers to the questions above and any other oral history notes you may have taken. Write two or three paragraphs on a separate piece of paper about the immigrant you interviewed.

61

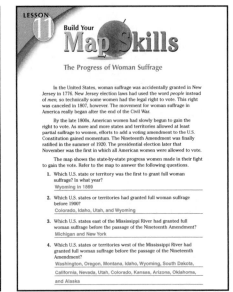

LESSON 11 — Build Your Map Skills

The Progress of Woman Suffrage

In the United States, woman suffrage was accidentally granted in New Jersey in 1776. New Jersey election laws had used the word *people* instead of *men*, so technically some women had the legal right to vote. This right was canceled in 1807, however. The movement for woman suffrage in America really began after the end of the Civil War.

By the late 1800s, American women had slowly begun to gain the right to vote. As more and more states and territories allowed at least partial suffrage to women, efforts to add a voting amendment to the U.S. Constitution gained momentum. The Nineteenth Amendment was finally ratified in the summer of 1920. The presidential election later that November was the first in which all American women were allowed to vote.

The map shows the state-by-state progress women made in their fight to gain the vote. Refer to the map to answer the following questions.

1. Which U.S. state or territory was the first to grant full woman suffrage? In what year?
   Wyoming in 1869

2. Which U.S. states or territories had granted full woman suffrage before 1900?
   Colorado, Idaho, Utah, and Wyoming

3. Which U.S. states east of the Mississippi River had granted full woman suffrage before the passage of the Nineteenth Amendment?
   Michigan and New York

4. Which U.S. states or territories west of the Mississippi River had granted full woman suffrage before the passage of the Nineteenth Amendment?
   Washington, Oregon, Montana, Idaho, Wyoming, South Dakota, California, Nevada, Utah, Colorado, Kansas, Arizona, Oklahoma, and Alaska

64

Answer Key

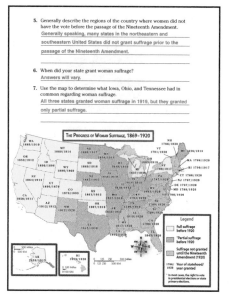

5. Generally describe the regions of the country where women did not have the vote before the passage of the Nineteenth Amendment.
Generally speaking, many states in the northeastern and southeastern United States did not grant suffrage prior to the passage of the Nineteenth Amendment.

6. When did your state grant woman suffrage?
Answers will vary.

7. Use the map to determine what Iowa, Ohio, and Tennessee had in common regarding woman suffrage.
All three states granted woman suffrage in 1919, but they granted only partial suffrage.

THE PROGRESS OF WOMAN SUFFRAGE, 1869–1920

65

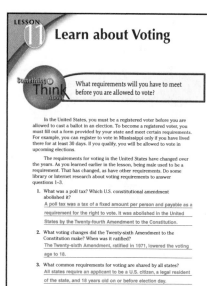

LESSON 11
Learn about Voting

Something to Think About
What requirements will you have to meet before you are allowed to vote?

In the United States, you must be a registered voter before you are allowed to cast a ballot in an election. To become a registered voter, you must fill out a form provided by your state and meet certain requirements. For example, you can register to vote in Mississippi only if you have lived there for at least 30 days. If you qualify, you will be allowed to vote in upcoming elections.

The requirements for voting in the United States have changed over the years. As you learned earlier in the lesson, being male used to be a requirement. That has changed, as have other requirements. Do some library or Internet research about voting requirements to answer questions 1–3.

1. What was a poll tax? Which U.S. constitutional amendment abolished it?
A poll tax was a tax of a fixed amount per person and payable as a requirement for the right to vote. It was abolished in the United States by the Twenty-fourth Amendment to the Constitution.

2. What voting changes did the Twenty-sixth Amendment to the Constitution make? When was it ratified?
The Twenty-sixth Amendment, ratified in 1971, lowered the voting age to 18.

3. What common requirements for voting are shared by all states?
All states require an applicant to be a U.S. citizen, a legal resident of the state, and 18 years old on or before election day.

66

The table below shows national voter turnout in federal elections since 1980. Use it to answer questions 4–6.

4. What percentage of the voting-age population actually cast a ballot in the 2004 presidential election?
In 2004, 55.3 percent voted.

5. Why do you think voter turnout tends to rise and fall in four-year cycles?
Possible answer: More people tend to vote in presidential election years because they consider it the most important election.

6. Generally speaking, has voter turnout been increasing or decreasing since 1980 as a percentage of the voting-age population?
Turnout as a percentage of the voting-age population has remained pretty much the same since 1980.

¹Year	Voting-age Population	Voter Registration	²Voter Turnout	Turnout of Voting-age Population (Percent)
2004	221,256,931	174,800,000	122,294,978	55.3
2002	215,473,000	150,990,598	79,830,119	37.0
2000	205,815,000	156,421,311	105,586,274	51.3
1998	200,929,000	141,850,558	73,117,022	36.4
1996	196,511,000	146,211,960	96,456,345	49.1
1994	193,650,000	130,292,822	75,105,860	38.8
1992	189,529,000	133,821,178	104,405,155	55.1
1990	185,812,000	121,105,630	67,859,189	36.5
1988	182,778,000	126,379,628	91,594,693	50.1
1986	178,566,000	118,399,984	64,991,128	36.4
1984	174,466,000	124,150,614	92,652,680	53.1
1982	169,938,000	110,671,225	67,615,576	39.8
1980	164,597,000	113,043,734	86,515,221	52.6

Voter Turnout in Federal Elections: 1980–2004

¹Data for elections in the colored rows, such as 2004, were for president and members of Congress; elections in other years, such as 2002, were for members of Congress only.
²Turnout refers to the number of voters who actually cast votes.

67

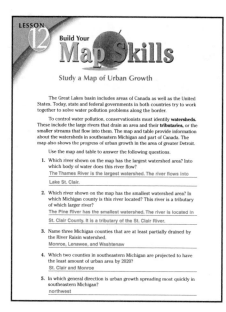

LESSON 12
Build Your Map Skills

Study a Map of Urban Growth

The Great Lakes basin includes areas of Canada as well as the United States. Today, state and federal governments in both countries try to work together to solve water pollution problems along the border.

To control water pollution, conservationists must identify **watersheds.** These include the large rivers that drain an area and their **tributaries,** or the smaller streams that flow into them. The map and table provide information about the watersheds in southeastern Michigan and part of Canada. The map also shows the progress of urban growth in the area of greater Detroit.

Use the map and table to answer the following questions.

1. Which river shown on the map has the largest watershed area? Into which body of water does this river flow?
The Thames River is the largest watershed. The river flows into Lake St. Clair.

2. Which river shown on the map has the smallest watershed area? In which Michigan county is this river located? This river is a tributary of which larger river?
The Pine River has the smallest watershed. The river is located in St. Clair County. It is a tributary of the St. Clair River.

3. Name three Michigan counties that are at least partially drained by the River Raisin watershed.
Monroe, Lenawee, and Washtenaw

4. Which two counties in southeastern Michigan are projected to have the least amount of urban area by 2020?
St. Clair and Monroe

5. In which general direction is urban growth spreading most quickly in southeastern Michigan?
northwest

70

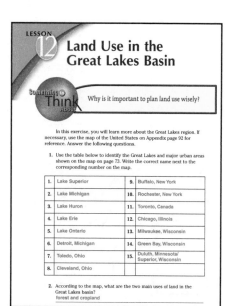

LESSON 12
Land Use in the Great Lakes Basin

Something to Think About
Why is it important to plan land use wisely?

In this exercise, you will learn more about the Great Lakes region. If necessary, use the map of the United States on Appendix page 92 for reference. Answer the following questions.

1. Use the table below to identify the Great Lakes and major urban areas shown on the map on page 73. Write the correct name next to the corresponding number on the map.

1.	Lake Superior	9.	Buffalo, New York
2.	Lake Michigan	10.	Rochester, New York
3.	Lake Huron	11.	Toronto, Canada
4.	Lake Erie	12.	Chicago, Illinois
5.	Lake Ontario	13.	Milwaukee, Wisconsin
6.	Detroit, Michigan	14.	Green Bay, Wisconsin
7.	Toledo, Ohio	15.	Duluth, Minnesota/ Superior, Wisconsin
8.	Cleveland, Ohio		

2. According to the map, what are the two main uses of land in the Great Lakes basin?
forest and cropland

72

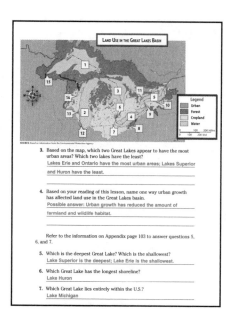

LAND USE IN THE GREAT LAKES BASIN

SOURCE: Based on information from the Environmental Protection Agency

3. Based on the map, which two Great Lakes appear to have the most urban areas? Which two lakes have the least?
Lakes Erie and Ontario have the most urban areas; Lakes Superior and Huron have the least.

4. Based on your reading of this lesson, name one way urban growth has affected land use in the Great Lakes basin.
Possible answer: Urban growth has reduced the amount of farmland and wildlife habitat.

Refer to the information on Appendix page 103 to answer questions 5, 6, and 7.

5. Which is the deepest Great Lake? Which is the shallowest?
Lake Superior is the deepest; Lake Erie is the shallowest.

6. Which Great Lake has the longest shoreline?
Lake Huron

7. Which Great Lake lies entirely within the U.S.?
Lake Michigan

73

Answer Key

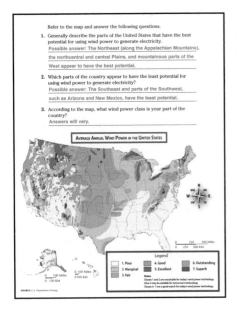

Refer to the map and answer the following questions.

1. Generally describe the parts of the United States that have the best potential for using wind power to generate electricity.
   Possible answer: The Northeast (along the Appalachian Mountains), the northcentral and central Plains, and mountainous parts of the West appear to have the best potential.

2. Which parts of the country appear to have the least potential for using wind power to generate electricity?
   Possible answer: The Southeast and parts of the Southwest, such as Arizona and New Mexico, have the least potential.

3. According to the map, what wind power class is your part of the country?
   Answers will vary.

77

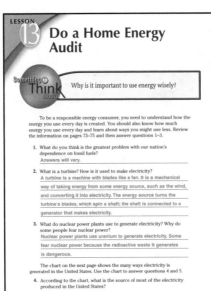

LESSON 13 — Do a Home Energy Audit

Something to Think About — Why is it important to use energy wisely?

To be a responsible energy consumer, you need to understand how the energy you use every day is created. You should also know how much energy you use every day and learn about ways you might use less. Review the information on pages 73–75 and then answer questions 1–3.

1. What do you think is the greatest problem with our nation's dependence on fossil fuels?
   Answers will vary.

2. What is a turbine? How is it used to make electricity?
   A turbine is a machine with blades like a fan. It is a mechanical way of taking energy from some energy source, such as the wind, and converting it into electricity. The energy source turns the turbine's blades, which spin a shaft; the shaft is connected to a generator that makes electricity.

3. What do nuclear power plants use to generate electricity? Why do some people fear nuclear power?
   Nuclear power plants use uranium to generate electricity. Some fear nuclear power because the radioactive waste it generates is dangerous.

The chart on the next page shows the many ways electricity is generated in the United States. Use the chart to answer questions 4 and 5.

4. According to the chart, what is the source of most of the electricity produced in the United States?
   coal

78

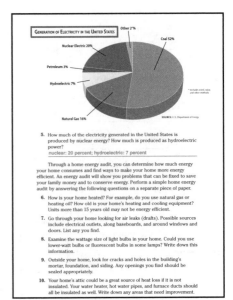

5. How much of the electricity generated in the United States is produced by nuclear energy? How much is produced as hydroelectric power?
   nuclear: 20 percent; hydroelectric: 7 percent

Through a home energy audit, you can determine how much energy your home consumes and find ways to make your home more energy efficient. An energy audit will show you problems that can be fixed to save your family money and to conserve energy. Perform a simple home energy audit by answering the following questions on a separate piece of paper.

6. How is your home heated? For example, do you use natural gas or heating oil? How old is your home's heating and cooling equipment? Units more than 15 years old may not be energy efficient.

7. Go through your home looking for air leaks (drafts). Possible sources include electrical outlets, along baseboards, and around windows and doors. List any you find.

8. Examine the wattage size of light bulbs in your home. Could you use lower-watt bulbs or fluorescent bulbs in some lamps? Write down this information.

9. Outside your home, look for cracks and holes in the building's mortar, foundation, and siding. Any openings you find should be sealed appropriately.

10. Your home's attic could be a great source of heat loss if it is not insulated. Your water heater, hot water pipes, and furnace ducts should all be insulated as well. Write down any areas that need improvement.

79

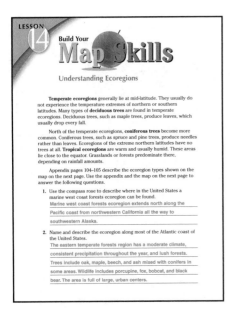

LESSON 14 — Build Your Map Skills
Understanding Ecoregions

Temperate ecoregions generally lie at mid-latitude. They usually do not experience the temperature extremes of northern or southern latitudes. Many types of **deciduous trees** are found in temperate ecoregions. Deciduous trees, such as maple trees, produce leaves, which usually drop every fall.

North of the temperate ecoregions, **coniferous trees** become more common. Coniferous trees, such as spruce and pine trees, produce needles rather than leaves. Ecoregions of the extreme northern latitudes have no trees at all. **Tropical ecoregions** are warm and usually humid. These areas lie close to the equator. Grasslands or forests predominate there, depending on rainfall amounts.

Appendix pages 104–105 describe the ecoregion types shown on the map on the next page. Use the appendix and the map on the next page to answer the following questions.

1. Use the compass rose to describe where in the United States a marine west coast forests ecoregion can be found.
   Marine west coast forests ecoregion extends north along the Pacific coast from northwestern California all the way to southwestern Alaska.

2. Name and describe the ecoregion along most of the Atlantic coast of the United States.
   The eastern temperate forests region has a moderate climate, consistent precipitation throughout the year, and lush forests. Trees include oak, maple, beech, and ash mixed with conifers in some areas. Wildlife includes porcupine, fox, bobcat, and black bear. The area is full of large, urban centers.

82

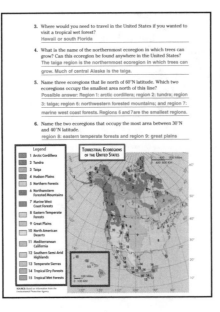

3. Where would you need to travel in the United States if you wanted to visit a tropical wet forest?
   Hawaii or south Florida

4. What is the name of the northernmost ecoregion in which trees can grow? Can this ecoregion be found anywhere in the United States?
   The taiga region is the northernmost ecoregion in which trees can grow. Much of central Alaska is the taiga.

5. Name three ecoregions that lie north of 60°N latitude. Which two ecoregions occupy the smallest area north of this line?
   Possible answer: Region 1: arctic cordillera; region 2: tundra; region 3: taiga; region 6: northwestern forested mountains; and region 7: marine west coast forests. Regions 6 and 7 are the smallest regions.

6. Name the two ecoregions that occupy the most area between 30°N and 40°N latitude.
   region 8: eastern temperate forests and region 9: great plains

83

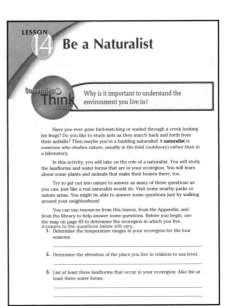

LESSON 14 — Be a Naturalist

Something to Think About — Why is it important to understand the environment you live in?

Have you ever gone bird-watching or waded through a creek looking for frogs? Do you like to study ants as they march back and forth from their anthills? Then maybe you're a budding naturalist! A **naturalist** is someone who studies nature, usually in the field (outdoors) rather than in a laboratory.

In this activity, you will take on the role of a naturalist. You will study the landforms and water forms that are in your ecoregion. You will learn about some plants and animals that make their homes there, too.

Try to get out into nature to answer as many of these questions as you can, just like a real naturalist would do. Visit some nearby parks or nature areas. You might be able to answer some questions just by walking around your neighborhood.

You can use resources from this lesson, from the Appendix, and from the library to help answer some questions. Before you begin, use the map on page 83 to determine the ecoregion in which you live.
Answers to the questions below will vary.

1. Determine the temperature ranges in your ecoregion for the four seasons.

2. Determine the elevation of the place you live in relation to sea level.

3. List at least three landforms that occur in your ecoregion. Also list at least three water forms.

84

Answer Key

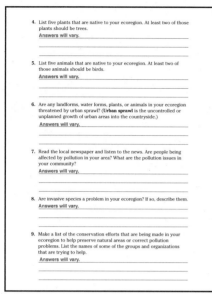

4. List five plants that are native to your ecoregion. At least two of those plants should be trees.
   Answers will vary.

5. List five animals that are native to your ecoregion. At least two of those animals should be birds.
   Answers will vary.

6. Are any landforms, water forms, plants, or animals in your ecoregion threatened by urban sprawl? (**Urban sprawl** is the uncontrolled or unplanned growth of urban areas into the countryside.)
   Answers will vary.

7. Read the local newspaper and listen to the news. Are people being affected by pollution in your area? What are the pollution issues in your community?
   Answers will vary.

8. Are invasive species a problem in your ecoregion? If so, describe them.
   Answers will vary.

9. Make a list of the conservation efforts that are being made in your ecoregion to help preserve natural areas or correct pollution problems. List the names of some of the groups and organizations that are trying to help.
   Answers will vary.

85

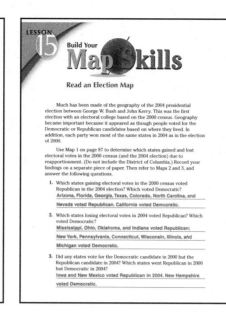

LESSON 15
Build Your Map Skills

Read an Election Map

Much has been made of the geography of the 2004 presidential election between George W. Bush and John Kerry. This was the first election with an electoral college based on the 2000 census. Geography became important because it appeared as though people voted for the Democratic or Republican candidates based on where they lived. In addition, each party won most of the same states in 2004 as in the election of 2000.

Use Map 1 on page 87 to determine which states gained and lost electoral votes in the 2000 census (and the 2004 election) due to reapportionment. (Do not include the District of Columbia.) Record your findings on a separate piece of paper. Then refer to Maps 2 and 3, and answer the following questions.

1. Which states gaining electoral votes in the 2000 census voted Republican in the 2004 election? Which voted Democratic?
   Arizona, Florida, Georgia, Texas, Colorado, North Carolina, and Nevada voted Republican. California voted Democratic.

2. Which states losing electoral votes in 2004 voted Republican? Which voted Democratic?
   Mississippi, Ohio, Oklahoma, and Indiana voted Republican; New York, Pennsylvania, Connecticut, Wisconsin, Illinois, and Michigan voted Democratic.

3. Did any states vote for the Democratic candidate in 2000 but the Republican candidate in 2004? Which states went Republican in 2000 but Democratic in 2004?
   Iowa and New Mexico voted Republican in 2004. New Hampshire voted Democratic.

88

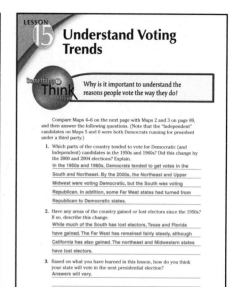

LESSON 15
Understand Voting Trends

Something to Think About

Why is it important to understand the reasons people vote the way they do?

Compare Maps 4–6 on the next page with Maps 2 and 3 on page 89, and then answer the following questions. (Note that the "Independent" candidates on Maps 5 and 6 were both Democrats running for president under a third party.)

1. Which parts of the country tended to vote for Democratic (and Independent) candidates in the 1950s and 1960s? Did this change by the 2000 and 2004 elections? Explain.
   In the 1950s and 1960s, Democrats tended to get votes in the South and Northeast. By the 2000s, the Northeast and Upper Midwest were voting Democratic, but the South was voting Republican. In addition, some Far West states had turned from Republican to Democratic states.

2. Have any areas of the country gained or lost electors since the 1950s? If so, describe this change.
   While much of the South has lost electors, Texas and Florida have gained. The Far West has remained fairly steady, although California has also gained. The northeast and Midwestern states have lost electors.

3. Based on what you have learned in this lesson, how do you think your state will vote in the next presidential election?
   Answers will vary.

90

Notes